MW00648859

Always Believe in Love

SELECTED WRITINGS OF ELIZABETH OF THE TRINITY

Always believe in love.
He loves you today,
As He loved you yesterday
And as He will love you tomorrow.

Elizabeth of the Trinity
Letter 298

Always Believe in Love

SELECTED WRITINGS OF ELIZABETH OF THE TRINITY

Compiled and Introduced
by Marian Murphy

ICS Publications
Institute of Carmelite Studies
Washington, D.C.

ICS Publications
2131 Lincoln Road NE
Washington, DC 20002-1199

www.icspublications.org

© Washington Province of Discalced Carmelites, Inc., 2017

Published with Ecclesiastical Approval

All rights reserved. No part of this book may be reproduced or transmitted in any form or by any means, electronic or mechanical, including photocopying, recording, or by any information, storage or retrieval system without prior written permission from the publisher.

Dedication
To my mother, Terri,
With all my love and gratitude

Cover photo and other photos of Elizabeth of the Trinity kindness of the Carmel of Dijon (Dijon-Flavignerot), published with permission

Cover design and typesetting by Rose Design
Produced and printed in the United States of America

Library of Congress Cataloging-in-Publication Data

Names: Elizabeth of the Trinity, Saint, 1880-1906, author. | Murphy, Marian Teresa, compiler.
Title: Always believe in love : selected writings of Elizabeth of the Trinity / compiled and introduced by Marian Murphy.
Description: First [edition]. | Washington, D.C. : ICS Publications, 2017. | Originally published: Hyde Park, N.Y. : New City Press, c2009. | Includes bibliographical references.
Identifiers: LCCN 2017012829 | ISBN 9781939272546 ((cu : alk. paper)
Subjects: LCSH: Mysticism--Catholic Church. | Spiritual life--Catholic Church. | Elizabeth of the Trinity, Saint, 1880-1906--Correspondence.
Classification: LCC BV5082.3 .E4513 2017 | DDC 271/.97102--dc23
LC record available at https://lccn.loc.gov/2017012829

ISBN 13 978-1-939272-54-6

10 9 8 7 6 5 4 3 2 1

Contents

Abbreviations

Writings of Elizabeth of the Trinity used in this book:

D = Diary
L = Letters
P = Poems

Introduction

W̲e study the saints in order to learn how to become better human beings: they teach us how to live, love, and
die worthily. The saints are God's glorious palette, and without them, as Gilbert Keith Chesterton said: "we could lose the
humanity of Christ"; for in them, we experience his rootedness
in our ordinary lives. Their passionate, single-minded following
of Christ fascinates us as we recognize the source of their, and
our, true greatness.

St. Elizabeth of the Trinity, Witness to Holiness

Why do we study St. Elizabeth of the Trinity in particular? At
first glance one might ask what the very short life of a Carmelite living a hundred years ago in France has to offer us. In his
homily for the beatification of Elizabeth of the Trinity, John
Paul II made some suggestions. Acknowledging her spiritual
influence on him, he presented her to the church as "a brilliant
witness of love and joy," a Carmelite prophet of the indwelling
presence of God; one who knew herself to be indwelt by the
Trinity of Love. By incarnating these Christian values in her
own unique way, Elizabeth reminds us that the experience of
the saints is not out of our reach, it is rather a paradigm for all
Christians. The sanctifying grace of baptism empowers us to
embrace our Christian vocation and the fullness of Elizabeth's
response offers a model for our journey from baptism to glory.
In her we see what we are each called to be.

Elizabeth lived twenty-one years of her life as a layperson
and only five in Carmel. She has much to say, therefore, to
people of all ages who desire intimacy with God amid involve-
ment in the world. Responding wholeheartedly to God's longing for each one of us, Elizabeth leads us anew to the absolute

center of Christian holiness, Christ himself. She expressed her longing thus: "Master, I want to be a saint for you; you be my sanctity."[1] Lest this sound too exalted it is important to remember that, essentially, Elizabeth lived an utterly practical spirituality. In faith, she saw that everything could be like a sacrament. This is "everyday mysticism" where nothing is trivial, and the ordinary becomes sacred. Elizabeth gives sound advice, rooted in the French spiritual tradition, which saw no gap between life and spirituality:

> Look at every suffering and every joy as coming directly from Him, and then your life will be a continual communion, since everything will be like a sacrament that will give you God. (L 264)

The Second Vatican Council rediscovered the universal call to holiness of all Christians, whatever their state in life, not as an option, but as an imperative: to be a follower of Christ means committing ourselves to holiness. In Leon Bloy's haunting words, "There is only one sadness, the sadness of not being a saint."

Elizabeth's Life

Faith perceives life's complex interweaving of happenings as a spiritual journey, and not merely a random concatenation of events. Biography is where *chronos* and *kairos* interact in the unique incarnation that is each one of us: for a believer, therefore, biography is spirituality.[2]

A Child of Contrasts: Affectionate and Volatile

Marie Joséphine Elizabeth Catez was born in an army camp in Avour near Bourges, central France, on Sunday, July 18, 1880,

1. Conrad De Meester, *Elisabeth de la Trinité: Oeuvres Complètes* (Paris: Editions du Cerf, 2002), 895.
2. Ronald Rolheiser, *Forgotten Among the Lilies* (Reading: Spire Books, 1990), 8.

the eldest of two daughters. Her father, Joseph Catez, was a courageous army captain, an esteemed chevalier of the Legion of Honor; her mother, Marie Rolland, was the daughter of a commandant. An affectionate child, Elizabeth had soldiers' blood in her veins and it showed in her fiery temperament which she struggled to overcome. Her temper was legendary and her mother almost despaired of her "real rages" and "furious eyes." It is a measure of Elizabeth's growth in grace that she will later be admired for her composure and serene gaze.

A Year of Grief and Growth

1887 was a year of grief for young Elizabeth as tears of rage turned to tears of sadness: her grandfather, Raymond Rolland, died in January and her father died of a heart attack in Elizabeth's arms, in October. These deaths precipitated a move to an apartment near Dijon Carmel. The double loss undoubtedly matured Elizabeth, impressing upon her the fragility of life. Around this time she confided her desire to be a nun to Canon Emelien Isidore Angles, a lifelong family friend and confidant. Her mother was shocked and disapproving and for the next fourteen years, Elizabeth's desire and her mother's opposition would clash, causing untold suffering to both. Elizabeth was torn between the "drama of two loves": the love of God and love of her mother whom she adored. Like a horizontal and vertical beam, they formed a cross in Elizabeth's heart, until her mother eventually consented.

This was also the year of Elizabeth's first confession, which she described as her "conversion." This appears startling when applied to one so young. Was Elizabeth perhaps referring to a "spiritual awakening," described in terms of conversion? It is clear, however, that her spiritual life begins with the conscious decision to respond to the grace of Christ at that time. A complex picture emerges during this period, suggesting an ongoing internal struggle: Elizabeth became noticeably more prayerful and made remarkable efforts to overcome her temper.

First Holy Communion

Elizabeth's First Holy Communion marked a further milestone on her spiritual journey. In a poem, *That Great Day*, written to commemorate her seventh anniversary, Elizabeth uses almost mystical terms, describing the experience as a "mysterious exchange," and "delightful encounter." Elizabeth's awareness of Jesus' real presence caused tears of joy which recall Gregory of Nyssa's words: "It is impossible for one to live without tears who considers things as they really are." From that moment, she said, "We gave ourselves to each other without words," the Lord took over her heart and the Eucharist became central to her life.

During a visit to Dijon Carmel that afternoon, Elizabeth was told that her name meant "House of the God of Love." Although etymologically inaccurate (it actually means "God has sworn") it was theologically true, for every Christian becomes a temple of God through baptism. The moral transformation begun at the age of seven was subsequently undertaken with greater seriousness as Elizabeth took responsibility for her spiritual growth. In Jungian language, she confronted her shadow. Elizabeth's baptismal faith began to develop into something "perfect and mature,"[3] manifesting how the Eucharist "sacramentalizes the solid and continuous possession of life begun in baptism and confirmation,"[4] opening her up to the sacramentality of everyday life.

Eucharist—Source of Holiness

In the Eucharist Elizabeth found the strength to recognize her faults, struggle against the uncomfortable weakness of her explosive nature and practice virtue. She fought passion with passion, replacing self-love with love of God. Her commitment to the "battle" (*aoratos polemos*) against her fierce anger and

---

3. *Catechism of the Catholic Church*, 1253.
4. Liam G. Walsh, *The Sacraments of Initiation* (London: Geoffrey Chapman, 1988), 265.

sensibilité bore fruit and others noted a gradual transformation. In her we see how Eucharistic sacramental encounter is the foundation of all Christian life, for we only live and flourish as Christians in and through the Eucharist.

The lives of the saints provide many examples of the receptivity of the young to the transforming effects of the Eucharist: Gemma Galgani, Dominic Savio, Aloysius Gonzaga, to name but a few. Elizabeth offers a model for catechizing the young and reminds us not to underestimate the power of God's grace in his "little ones." Our cynical age needs to rediscover the simplicity of God's chosen ones, and their confidence in the Eucharist. Elizabeth was learning through the Eucharist, "the school of the saints," and the "source and summit" of Christian life.[5] In Augustine's words, in the Eucharist we "receive what we are" and are called to "become what we celebrate."[6] Sacramental liturgy celebrates the core insight that spirituality is essentially a matter of ongoing growth in holiness through conformity to Christ. Through the Eucharist Elizabeth grew in prayer and holiness of life, combining asceticism and active charity.

Eucharistic Graces—Vocation

Around the age of fourteen, two significant vocational "moments" occurred in the context of the Eucharist, during Elizabeth's moment of prayer after Holy Communion. The first she described as being irresistibly drawn to choose Jesus as her only spouse, so that without delay she bound herself to him by a vow of virginity. No words were spoken, "but we gave ourselves to each other with such an intense love that the determination to be wholly His became even stronger."[7]

---

5. *Lumen Gentium*, 11. See John Paul II, *Ecclesia de Eucharistia*, 6.

6. See Rolheiser, 164.

7. Archives of Dijon Carmel (1906): *Sr. Elizabeth of the Trinity's Death Circular*, Private Publication, 2.

The second Eucharistic "moment" clarified the form of Elizabeth's religious vocation. She had been considering entering the Trappistines, attracted by their strict rule of silence. However, once, during her thanksgiving after Holy Communion, she had "heard the word *Carmel* pronounced within [her] soul" her only desire was to become a Carmelite.[8] Thus began possibly the most difficult and spiritually formative period of Elizabeth's life: she desperately wanted to enter Carmel but her mother withheld her consent.

Elizabeth in Exile

In one of life's ironies, Elizabeth's mother, a lifelong devotee of St. Teresa of Avila, totally opposed her daughter's vocation to the Teresian Carmel. Thus prevented from entering Carmel, Elizabeth courageously followed her Carmelite vocation initially alone, then, from 1899, as a "postulant outside the walls." Living as a Carmelite "in the world," Elizabeth helped to prepare the chapel of Dijon Carmel for feasts; participated in the liturgy and generally helped the extern sisters[9] with other aspiring Carmelites. Instead of Elizabeth being hidden in a cell in Carmel, Carmel was hidden in "the cell of her heart."

Elizabeth described this desert period as a time of "exile," during which she submitted to God's will. Grasping the secret of mature spirituality, in the darkness of faith, she recognized that there are no accidents or interruptions in life. Through wholeheartedly embracing this painful reality, this long period of waiting became one of the most spiritually productive of her life. Unable to enter Carmel she chose to make the long "journey inward" which is, in fact, the essence of the spiritual journey. In a push-button society of instant gratification,

---

8. Dijon Carmel, Benedictine of Stanbrook Abbey, trans., *Reminiscences of Sr. Elizabeth of the Trinity Servant of God* (Cork: Mercier Press, 1913), 17.

9. Carmelites who live outside enclosure, acting as a link between the enclosed nuns and the outside world.

we have forgotten the important art of *wu-wei*, waiting in "non-action," of living "the sublime fire of tension."[10] This is a potent message for today's world: learning to wait on life, on God. Elizabeth's resulting serenity recalls the inner tranquility of the desert Fathers, achieved through dying to self and focusing totally on Jesus.

Contemplative in the Midst of the World

Elizabeth provides an attractive model for those who live in the world but not submerged by some of its questionable values. She eloquently witnesses to the fact that it is not where we are but the direction in which we are traveling that matters. Full of life and vitality, she loved clothes and, a talented dressmaker, was adept at reproducing Paris fashions. An accomplished pianist and dancer, Elizabeth's sparkling personality made her popular at soirees and her affectionate and sensitive nature made her a valued friend. People also noted her "luminous gaze" and its source, her life of deep prayer and asceticism. Cardinal John Henry Newman urged Christians to recognize the "beauty of holiness" and it was evident in Elizabeth. We are given an indirect insight into Elizabeth's spiritual growth during this period in eight letters written by her from Carmel to Germaine de Gemeaux, whose situation mirrored Elizabeth's insofar as Germaine's mother also resisted her Carmelite vocation. Elizabeth reassured Germaine that she could already live as a Carmelite, because "Jesus knows the Carmelite by what is *within* her, by her soul" (L 133).

Carmel at Last—Joy, Turmoil, Prayer to the Trinity

Elizabeth entered the Carmel of Dijon on August 2, 1901, two weeks after her twenty-first birthday, becoming Sister Marie Elizabeth of the Trinity. Her spiritual maturity was so marked that a sister wrote in a letter to Lisieux Carmel: "Our postulant . . . will

---

10. Rolheiser, *Against an Infinite Horizon* (London: Hodder & Stoughton, 1995), 44.

become a saint for she already has remarkable disposition for it." After her postulancy of four months, which Elizabeth found "delightful," she was overjoyed to receive the Carmelite habit on the feast of the Immaculate Conception, December 8, 1901.

In contrast to the light and joy of her postulancy, the novitiate was characterized by interior darkness and suffering. Mother Germaine of Jesus, Elizabeth's prioress, novice mistress, and first biographer gives no details, only referring in Elizabeth's obituary to dryness in prayer, spiritual darkness, scruples, anxieties, and depression. Elizabeth's physical health suffered and her dominant fault, hypersensitivity, resurfaced, causing Elizabeth great distress after all her efforts to overcome herself. She had become a very holy young woman before entering, but she had to learn to be a holy nun. With characteristic faith and generosity Elizabeth endured, and was solemnly professed on the feast of the Epiphany, January 11, 1903.

Inner peace returned and Sister Elizabeth of the Trinity entered into the "mystery and whole vocation in [her] name," which proved central to her spirituality. The most profound and famous expression of her understanding of this central Christian mystery is her *Prayer to the Trinity*, which conveys her almost palpable intimacy with "the Three" and leads us into our own relationship with the indwelling Trinity. The church implicitly recognizes this in citing Elizabeth's *Prayer to the Trinity* as the culminating expression of the section on the Trinity in the *New Catechism*.[11] Her *Trinity Prayer* "speaks" her soul, the church's and, if we open ourselves up to it, ours.

"Praise of His Glory"

Elizabeth's spiritual life developed further when she received a profound personal grace, after reading Paul's Letter to the Ephesians, 1:12.

---

11. *Catechism of the Catholic Church*, 260.

We who first hoped in Christ have been
Destined and appointed to live for the praise of his glory.

Through this, she received the grace of her personal vocation, to live as a "Praise of God's Glory." She understood this
to be her "new name" (Rev 2:17). Many themes merge in this
outpouring of her spirit: her desire to live in union with the
Trinity, in order to be holy and an apostle of love in the Church,
thus becoming the "Praise of Glory of the Trinity." She shared
her discovery with Canon Angles: "I am going to tell you a
very personal secret: my dream is to be 'the praise of his glory.'
I read that in St. Paul and my bridegroom made me understand that this was to be my vocation while in exile, waiting to
sing the eternal *Sanctus* in the City of the saints" (L 256).

While Elizabeth blossomed spiritually, physically her
health deteriorated noticeably as Addison's disease took hold.
Lent 1905 was a terrible struggle, and she felt constantly
exhausted. By August she had been relieved of her duties at
the turn and given time in the garden in the hope that the
fresh air might restore her. To no avail. As her health declined,
her spirit soared as she delighted in St. Paul's writings, rel-
ishing the wonder of being *Laudem Gloriae*. Perhaps the "new
name," as so often in Scripture, indicated a change of direction: in this instance, toward Calvary.

The Road to Calvary: March–November 1906

As early as 1903, Elizabeth had been diagnosed as suffering
from Addison's disease, which at that time was incurable. The
symptoms were painful and distressing: loss of appetite and
weight, exhaustion, severe headaches, insomnia, stomach dis-
orders, and finally death.

Elizabeth's health deteriorated rapidly in Lent 1906, and
she was moved to the infirmary. It is impossible to describe
briefly the excruciating suffering Elizabeth endured in the last

eight months of her life or her incredible strength and faith. Mother Marie of Jesus, then prioress at Paray-le-Monial, made a last visit to Dijon Carmel and wrote to her community:

> I have had a beautiful sermon coming in contact with Sister Elizabeth of the Trinity. The little sister is a real saint: she speaks of her approaching death with a lovely simplicity, a joyous serenity and peace, and lives in the anticipation of God, in perfect surrender and love. She seems to be already in the retreat of eternity.[12]

This testimony recalls that it is life, especially at the point of death, which speaks most powerfully to us. Elizabeth knew she was dying. Like all last words, knowingly suffused with the light of eternity, hers are an "especially fascinating" spiritual testament for "what we say in the face of imminent silence" has unique power.[13] For Hans Urs von Balthasar, Elizabeth's earlier writings were "preparation and beginnings. In her final writings, her word is 'pure and flawless before God.'"[14] In early August, Elizabeth composed a ten-day retreat, *Heaven in Faith*, as a "souvenir" for her sister, Guite. She then made her own retreat, her "novitiate for heaven," The *Last Retreat of Laudem Gloriae*. These, along with *Greatness of Our Vocation*, and *Let Yourself Be Loved*, have been described as a "little *summa*."[15]

God was working on his loving servant to the very end. Mother Marie of Jesus told her sisters that Elizabeth's likeness to Christ was made visible in her very body which had become so emaciated as to be almost unrecognizable, reminding one of Jesus after he had been taken down from the cross. The words

---

12. M. E. Arendup, trans., *A Carmelite of the Sacred Heart: The Life of Mother Marie of Jesus* (London: Burns Oates & Washbourne, 1923), 144.

13. Timothy Radcliffe, *Seven Last Words* (London: Burns & Oates, 2004), 3.

14. Hans Urs von Balthasar, *Two Sisters in the Spirit: Thérèse of Lisieux and Elizabeth of the Trinity* (San Francisco: Ignatius Press, 1992), 383.

15. M. M. Philipon, *The Spiritual Doctrine of Sr. Elizabeth of the Trinity* (Cork: Mercier Press, 1947), 58.

of St. Paul, engraved on her profession crucifix, were written on her life and on her body: "I live, no longer I, but Christ lives in me." Elizabeth died around 6:15 a.m. on November 9. Her last intelligible words were, "I am going to light, to love, and to life." Elizabeth was beatified by Pope John Paul II, on November 24, 1984, and canonized by Pope Francis on October 16, 2016.

Elizabeth's "Secret"

According to Evagrius, "If you are a theologian you will really pray and if you really pray, you are a theologian."[16] Although Elizabeth never studied theology, she intuitively perceived the mystical depths of God in prayer where the Holy Spirit "gave witness to Himself" in her. She felt compelled to share this good news with others and there is a sense of increasing urgency in communicating her spiritual insights during the last six months of her life, manifested in the accumulation of metaphors she used to convey her message. The first, "my doctrine," occurs in May 1906 and is soon followed by references to: "grace," "recipe," "ideal," and "testament." Her favorite expression, "secret," occurs in numerous contexts from her earliest years in Carmel, demonstrating her psychological astuteness: Doesn't everyone want to know a "secret"? What is her "secret"?

"Heaven on Earth"

Elizabeth intuitively grasped key aspects of faith, particularly the reality of the presence of God: "There, in the depths of my heart, in the Heaven of my soul, I love to find Him, since He never leaves me. 'God in me, I in Him.' Oh, that is my life!" (L 62). From the moment of her First Holy Communion, Elizabeth felt dwelt in. Her sense of the profound reality of God's presence developed into an intimate relationship with the Trinity

---

16. See Benedict J. Groeschel, *Spiritual Passages: The Psychology of Spiritual Development* (New York: Crossroad, 1983), 123; Philipon, 159.

of Love, "my Three" which was the center of her life. From the silence and prayer of Carmel, which she refers to as an "anticipated Heaven," she shares one of her most beautiful insights:

> I have found my Heaven on earth, since Heaven is God, and God is in my soul. The day I understood this everything became clear to me. I would like to whisper this secret to those I love so they too might always cling to God through everything. (L 122)

We hear echoes of Jesus' words, so valued by St. Teresa of Avila in her spiritual classic, *The Way of Perfection*: "the kingdom of heaven is within you."[17] Elizabeth longs to communicate the wonder of this reality so that we may all know, love, and enjoy the indwelling presence of God: "Through everything we see Him for we bear Him within us, and our life is an anticipated Heaven. I ask God to teach you all these secrets" (L 123). Her experience is possible for every Christian, if we only open ourselves to the presence of God, and Elizabeth tells us how.

Intimacy with the Indwelling God

Only eleven days before her death, Elizabeth wrote that her mission in heaven would be to draw souls to God by helping them transcend themselves in order to cling to him in simplicity, silence, and recollection, thus allowing God to transform them into himself (L 335). She constantly urged others to forget themselves, to overcome self-preoccupation, "go out of themselves," thus creating an inner silence wherein God would make his indwelling presence felt in an intimate "mysterious exchange" between Lover and Beloved. Only in recollected lives can we experience this presence of God which transforms us into Christ, the goal of the Christian journey.

---

17. See *The Way of Perfection*, Chapter 28 in Kieran Kavanaugh and Otilio Rodriguez, trans., *The Collected Works of St. Teresa of Avila, Vol II* (Washington: ICS, 1980).

"Always Believe in His Love" *The French spirituality*

Chesterton said that if he could give only one sermon, it would be on pride; Elizabeth's would be on love. Rooted in the French school of spirituality, which gave us the devotion to the Sacred Heart, symbol of God's love, Elizabeth grasps the essential, that God is love.

Elizabeth recognized her own great capacity to love when she started reading the "magnificent epistles" of St. Paul, whom she called the "Father of my soul." Elizabeth, like St. Paul, was so enthralled by God's love that the words "God has loved us exceedingly" (see Eph 2:4) were like a "summary" of her life which could have been written on each moment. She was wholly absorbed by God's "exceeding love" and writes often of how her heart expanded through contact with the God who is all love. As it was for St. Bernard and many mystics, to "believe the love God has for us" (1 Jn 4:16) was absolutely central to Elizabeth's spirituality. For her, believing in God's love is "our great act of faith." How refreshing it is to have faith presented in terms of a loving relationship. In one of her last letters to Guite, her beloved younger sister, Elizabeth urged:

> Always believe in His love. He loves you today as He loved you yesterday and as He will love you tomorrow. (L 298)

Elizabeth reminds us that the Christian life begins and ends with being loved, for, as Pope Benedict XVI wrote, "Only being loved is being saved."[18] The deepest source of the joy which Elizabeth radiated and the foundation of her totally positive spirituality is the conviction that God loved her exceedingly. Not to be loved is the greatest of human tragedies, leading to aggressive behavior that is destructive of self and society. In contrast, to know and live in the utter certainty of God's love is the greatest

---

18. Joseph Ratzinger (Pope Benedict XVI), *"In the Beginning . . .": A Catholic Understanding of Creation and the Fall* (Grand Rapids, Mich.: Wm B. Eerdmans), 74.

gift anyone could receive and generates positive relationships and productive activity in all areas of our lives.

The Trinity as "Tout Amour"

God is a Trinity because God is love. The Trinity is the fullness of love, relationship, communion. Love is not what God has or does, but what God is. Elizabeth first described God as *"Tout Amour,"* "All Love," in a poem written for the feast of the Sacred Heart, when she was nearly eighteen. Her experience of God's love permeated her life and writings. It was so personal and intimate that, from the way God gave himself to her, it was as if He had only her to love and think about. She felt that the Triune God loved her deeply and personally; her experience recalls the poet Herbert's words, which are true for each of us,

> My God, what is a heart,
> That thou shouldst it so eye, and woo,
> Pouring upon it all thy art,
> As if thou hadst nothing else to do?[19]

A favorite saying of the Dijon Carmelites was, "I am sought, I am loved." Elizabeth loved to "lose" herself in the abyss of the Trinity of love and her *Prayer to the Trinity* immerses us in the mystery of the Trinity of Love.

Prayer in the "Cell of Our Heart"

Elizabeth loved Catherine of Siena's idea of creating an inner "cell of the heart," a silent inner space where we dwell with God in prayer. Elizabeth enthusiastically recommends this practice to all her correspondents whatever their state in life, priests, busy young mothers, the infirm: to enter the presence

---

19. Philip Sheldrake, *Love Took My Hand: The Spirituality of George Herbert* (New York: Cowley, 2000), 33. See also Peter G. van Breemen, *As Bread That Is Broken* (Denville, N.J.: Dimension Books,1974), 14ff.

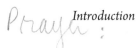

of God within. Prayer, for Elizabeth, was a heart-to-heart with a loving God, recalling Cardinal Newman's motto: *cor ad cor loqui-tur* (heart speaks to heart). She gave lots of practical advice on prayer, suggesting that rather than saying many vocal prayers, prayer is simply being with God, just being ourselves. Elizabeth loved St. Thérèse's little way of complete confidence in God, and recommended that we throw ourselves into the arms of God, with the loving abandonment of a little child. Prayer is not complicated; it is simply taking time to be alone with the Alone, the God who loves us unreservedly, just as we are; it is "rest and relaxation" as we let ourselves be loved by him.

Elizabeth's Style and Language

Elizabeth's style and language have been alternately praised and damned. Von Balthasar and Louis Bouyer praise Elizabeth's thought, but are less happy with her expression. Readers can judge for themselves, remembering that Elizabeth's writings were intended for specific individuals with no thought of publication: two of her most beautiful pieces, *Prayer to the Trinity* and *Let Yourself be Loved*, were only discovered after her death. Elizabeth's *Diary*, intended for no eyes but her own, is that of a fervent, idealistic young woman, passionate about God and her religious vocation. Her poems have little literary value; their significance lies, rather, in opening up for us her inner thoughts and deep feelings, providing us with a record of her spiritual journey. A study of her letters and retreats reveals Elizabeth's extensive use of her favorite writers, so much so that, after reading *Heaven in Faith*, Mother Germaine asked Elizabeth to use her own words when making notes on her *Last Retreat*. Only twenty-six when she died, Elizabeth showed considerable literary potential, evident in many of the passages selected for this anthology. While her style had not matured into her own "voice," the characteristic depth, vitality of thought, and spirituality make engaging reading.

Concluding Thoughts

Although Elizabeth of the Trinity was called to the very specific way of life of an enclosed contemplative Carmelite religious, this can only be adequately understood, in itself and in its relevance for others, in the context of the Christian understanding of our shared human vocation to holiness. In fact, Elizabeth's life and message are relevant for all Christians. In her letters from Carmel, Elizabeth conveys a sense of "eternal responsibility" for others. As St. John Paul II proclaimed, "far from isolating herself," she communicated her passion for God to her family, friends, and Carmelite sisters. God gifted her with a unique vocation in the church, to reveal a wonderful insight into our Christian calling. Cardinal Albert de Courtray, former Bishop of Dijon, expressed it succinctly:

> It is easy to see how Elizabeth's message is addressed to all Christians. She never for one moment entertained the idea that her calling as a Carmelite conferred some sort of spiritual superiority on her. For Christian spiritual life is founded upon faith, baptism and becoming ever more like Jesus Christ; so that whatever the Christian may be, whatever his or her moral, psychological or social condition, he or she is always that "new humanity" in which Christ will come again to renew all his mystery.[20]

Elizabeth of the Trinity invites us to dwell with the Triune God in our innermost depths. There, in the silence of faith and recollection we discover the secret of lasting happiness, letting ourselves be loved by the God of light, love, and life.

Sabette movie

---

20. Carmel de Dijon, Élisabeth de la Trinité: *Un Amour Excessif; Elizabeth of the Trinity, Boundless Love* (2006), DVD.

Extracts from Her Diary

1899–1900

Left: Nearly two years old; Elizabeth's passionate and choleric temperament was already evident.

Right: First Holy Communion, "The most beautiful day of my life."

Introduction

Elizabeth destroyed the first two notebooks of her Diary before enter-ing Carmel. Only the third and fourth remain, covering the brief yet significant period of 1899–1900. Her notes give a valuable insight into the catechesis of that period and faithfully record the four-week mission at Dijon, in Lent 1899, preached simultaneously in all the parishes. In terms of Elizabeth's spiritual journey, the Diary reveals her intensifying longing to give herself wholly to God in Carmel and the suffering caused to both mother and daughter by Madame Catez's resistance. Canon Angles, confidant to mother and daughter, spoke of Elizabeth's crucifying struggle, caught between the "drama of two loves," God and her mother.

By the age of eighteen Elizabeth had succeeded in controlling her difficult temperament. However, here she reveals the intensity of her sensitivity and just what it cost her.

"I felt my blood boiling"

It seems to me that when someone makes a comment which seems unjust, I feel my blood boiling in my veins and my whole being is in revolt! Today I had the joy of offering my Jesus several sacrifices regarding my dominant fault, but how much they cost me! I recognize my weakness there, but Jesus was with me. I heard His voice in the depths of my heart and then I was ready to endure everything for love of Him!

(D 1, January 1899)

There is a poignancy about this brief but telling entry, written on the feast of the Purification of Our Lady. Despite her own purifying suf-fering, Elizabeth renews her consecration to her "good Mother" Mary and her commitment to God's will while resolving to live as a "Carmel-ite in the world."

"May His will be done!"

Since Jesus does not want me, may His will be done! Let me become holy in the world: may nothing in it keep me from Him, may the trifles of earth neither preoccupy nor distract me. I am the bride of Jesus; we are so intimately united that nothing can separate us. Ah! May I always be worthy of my Heavenly Bridegroom; may I not squander His graces and may I have the happiness of proving how much I love Him.

(D 2, 2 February 1899)

Madame Catez, a lifelong devotee of St. Teresa of Avila, introduced her daughter to the teachings of the foundress of Carmel. St. Teresa's influence on Elizabeth's understanding of prayer and the spiritual life grew through her reading The Way of Perfection.

"How I love the way St. Teresa . . .
speaks of contemplation"

How I love the way St. Teresa treats this subject, when she speaks of contemplation, that degree of prayer in which God acts in us, uniting our soul so intimately to Himself that we no longer live, but it is He living in us. . . . I recognize there the delightful hours which the Divine Master has deigned to grant me during this retreat and often since then. What return can I make to Him for such great gifts? After these "little ecstasies" where the soul completely forgets herself and sees only her God, how hard and difficult ordinary prayer seems; how laborious it is to gather together one's powers; how much it costs and how difficult it seems!

(D 14, 2 February 1899)

After reading St. Teresa's advice on friendship, Elizabeth recognizes her need for detachment in order to focus all her affections on her Beloved.

"I have loved creatures too much"

O my Jesus, yes, I see that I have loved creatures too much; I have been too given over to them and have desired their affection too much, or rather I have not loved them with a divine love. But now I realize that I owe all my love to You, Beloved of my heart, and want only to be loved by You.

(D 15, 2 February1899)

Although only eighteen, Elizabeth is as good as her word and, under the guidance of her confessor and spiritual director, Abbé Gomard, she resolves to follow the way of interior mortification of the will, inspired by the motto of St. Ignatius of Loyola: "agenda contra" and "to go against" her self-will in all things.

"It is absolutely vital that I oppose my will
in everything, at all times"

My director spoke to me today of interior mortification; God clearly inspired him because I have been working on this since the retreat. I must convince myself that the bodily suffering to which I aspire is nothing but a means, however excellent, of reaching that interior mortification and complete detachment from myself. Jesus, my Love, my Life, help me; it is absolutely vital that I oppose my will in everything, at all times. Good Master, I immolate this will to You; make it one with yours. I promise You that I will make every effort to be faithful to this resolution to renounce my will in everything. It won't be easy, but with You, O my Strength and my Life, is victory not assured?

(D 16, 24 February 1899)

Elizabeth was also influenced by another great Carmelite's writing, St. Thérèse of Lisieux's autobiography and imitated her apostolic passion for the salvation of souls, praying for the conversion of her landlord, Monsieur Henri Chapuis.

"I would try every means to win back
this soul for Him"

When Jesus entered my heart this morning I told Him
that, with His help, I would try every means to win back this
soul for Him. I cannot sleep at night thinking about it; O heavenly Father, will you not be moved to pity? I am ready to do
anything to convert Monsieur Chapuis; give him to me and
let me endure any torments he has deserved. I will bear them
all for my Jesus, with my Jesus. May this sinner not let this
mission, this moment of great mercy pass by without profiting
from it and returning to you. My heart is breaking; O my God,
hear my prayer! Whenever I feel any pain, I rejoice and say to
myself, "Mary has heard my prayer; yes, yes, she will do it; I
expect a miracle!"

(D 74, 19 March 1899)

*On Palm Sunday, Guite raises the subject of Elizabeth's Carmelite
vocation with their mother and Madame Catez finally gives Elizabeth
permission to enter Carmel, but only in two years, when she will be
twenty-one. Although Elizabeth has been longing for this moment, she
is torn between joy and sadness. She records the occasion in her Diary,
and, despite writing that she is "lost for words," composes a twenty-nine
stanza poem, her longest by far.*

"In the midst of my suffering I feel
an infinite peace"

Marguerite once more spoke to mother about my vocation;
but mother said she thought that I was no longer considering it because I hadn't spoken about it. After dinner, my poor
little mother questioned me, and when she saw that I hadn't
changed my mind, she cried a lot and told me that she would
not stop me from going when I was twenty-one; that I would
only have two years to wait and that, in conscience, I could not
leave my sister before then.

Oh, how I admire her resignation! It is truly Mary who has obtained this grace, for I had not seen it in that way before. When I saw them both crying for me, my tears started to flow! My Jesus, if it were not You who were calling me and supporting me, if I could not see You holding Your arms over my loved ones, my heart would break. I would do anything to prevent them shedding a single tear, yet I am the cause of their sufferings. O my Master, I know You want me and You give me the strength and courage I need: in the midst of my suffering I feel an infinite peace. Yes, soon I'll be able to answer Your call. During these two years I am going to try even harder to make of myself a bride less unworthy of You, my Beloved.

I must be dreaming! It is too good to be true! I cannot believe that You have kept such happiness for me, such a poor, miserable creature. May You be forever blessed! And now, O You who can fill my heart, burn and tear out everything in me that displeases You! O Mary, I thank you! Continue your work in me; sustain my beloved mother whose courage I so admire; reward my dear little sister who only thinks of my happiness. Give them strength and courage. Help them to understand that, despite my love for them, I am ready to leave them for my Jesus. Let them recognize that it is He who is calling me, and that it is for Him alone that I sacrifice them. O, my Beloved, support them, support also her who is dying of love of You and who can find no words fitting enough to thank you!

(D 105, 26 March 1899, Palm Sunday)

Barely six days later, Madame Catez enthuses over a "superb marriage proposal." Elizabeth, with her charm, beauty, and intelligence would have been very eligible. She even danced with the future bishop of Montpellier! Elizabeth's diary entry dramatizes her feelings as an intimate dialogue between herself and Jesus. The conversations with her mother would have been particularly painful, as she only reluctantly consented to Elizabeth entering Carmel, hoping she would change her mind.

"A superb match . . . I am wholly Yours, uphold me"

Oh, Jesus, guard my heart; it is all Yours; I have already given it totally to You; it no longer belongs to me. This morning Mama returned very late and was quite excited. Someone had spoken to her about a marriage offer for me, a superb match that I would never find again. She discussed it with my confessor who advised her to speak to me of the advantages of such a match, saying it would be a good test for me, and that I ought to consider it carefully. He could not comment on it, but no interview was to be arranged without my consent. . . . How indifferent I am to this attractive proposal! My heart is no longer free; I can no longer dispose of it for I have given it to the King of kings.

I hear the voice of my Beloved in the depths of my heart: "My Bride," He says to me, "You refuse all this happiness here below in order to follow Me through sorrow and the Cross. You will have much suffering to endure and if I were not there to sustain you, you would find it unbearable. Even spiritual consolations which bring sweetness to the soul will be withdrawn from you. What trials those who follow me have to bear? But also, what sweetness and joys will I make you taste in your sufferings! I have chosen the best part for you, because I love you so much. Do you love your Jesus enough to accept these sufferings? Do you want to console Me? I am so abandoned, my daughter, do not leave Me alone. I want your heart. I love it. I have chosen it for Me. Keep your heart for Me!"

Yes, my Love, my Life, Beloved Spouse whom I adore; yes, I am ready to follow You along this way of sacrifices. You want to show me all the difficulties that I will encounter, Good Jesus; we will pass through them together; following You, with You, I will be strong. Oh, thank You for having chosen a poor creature like me to console You. You know well that I will never abandon You, for then I would be more guilty than those who crucified You twenty centuries ago. O, Supreme Love, I am wholly Yours; uphold me, because without You I am capable of any baseness, any crime. My mother is admirable; it is a miracle worked by Mary; for mother does not even try to shake my resolution. When she asked me to think things over, I told her that my response would be exactly the same in eight days, although I would willingly wait and give my answer then, if she wished it. . . . She understands me at last! "It would have been a comfort to me," she replied, "but God wills it otherwise. May His will be done."

(D 124, 31 March 1899, Good Friday)

Written eighteen months before entering Carmel, this extract shows how, in the words of the Dalai Lama's autobiography, Elizabeth also found "freedom in exile." In the desert, she reached new depths of interiority and surrender, that "pure point of dependence" on God which reaches the very core of one's being: to want only what God wants. In this supreme act of freedom Elizabeth offered her will entirely to God, achieving the "unum necessarium," *the "one thing necessary," that single-mindedness which Ignatius deemed the primary principle of spiritual growth. Elizabeth's anguish was intensified by the departure of her best friend, Marie-Louise Hallo, who was entering the novitiate of the Sacred Heart Sisters at Conflans.*

"I have surrendered all to Him, even my dearest desire . . ."

I have given myself to the good Master. . . . I have surrendered all to Him, even my dearest desire [to enter Carmel]. I only will what He wills; let Him take me when He chooses!

I have made the same resolutions this year: humility and self-renunciation, which include everything, and I ask Jesus to help me to keep them faithfully. Yes, my Beloved, I promise You that I will humble myself whenever the opportunity presents itself.

After these days spent in recollection, I cannot express the sadness which overwhelms me at the thought of going back to ordinary life again. I offer You this suffering, O Master; I am ready to do whatever You ask, and follow whatever path You choose.

(D 151, January 1900)

The final entry in Elizabeth's Diary is a plea for the gift of unceasing recollection and intimacy with her Master, which conveys the depth of Elizabeth's spirituality. Friends attest to her love of prayer. She rose early to pray, hiding spent matches to prevent her mother finding out; she also spent hours before the Blessed Sacrament. At this stage, Elizabeth had already received her name in Carmel, "Elizabeth of the Trinity," initially a disappointment as she so wanted to be called Elizabeth of Jesus. However, as she conveys in L 62, she has an incipient awareness of the "special vocation" in her name, which moves her to "delight in the mystery of the Blessed Trinity" as she loses herself in its depths.

"Let my life be a continual prayer"

My Divine Master, let my life be a continual prayer; let nothing, nothing distract me from You, neither work nor pleasures nor sufferings. May I be immersed in You.

In five days Marie-Louise is going to leave everything for You, I give her to You thanking You that you have chosen both of us as Your brides. I would love to be able to respond to Your call, but the hour has not yet come. May the holy will of God be always mine. . . . Yes, Lord, may Your will be done. I can belong to You even in the world. Then take my whole being; may Elizabeth disappear, and only Jesus remain.

(D 155, January 1900)

Letters

Left: 13–14 years old; Elizabeth's composure is evident.

Right: 14 years old; first prize for piano at Dijon Conservatory.

Introduction

Elizabeth of the Trinity was an enthusiastic letter writer and over 346 of her letters to family and friends have been preserved. Before entering Carmel, she wrote to friends while she was away on holiday. After entering, Elizabeth's correspondence increased. Her correspondents included six priests and seminarians, thirteen religious, and thirty-one lay people.

Her letters reveal Elizabeth's deeply affectionate nature which becomes, if possible, more loving when she enters Carmel. She calls everyone "mama": Madame Hallo, her next door neighbor, is a "second mama" and she is her "second daughter." She writes similarly to Madame de Sourdon and Madame de Gemeaux. All her friends are "sisters" and Charles Hallo, to whom she wrote her last letter, is "my little brother." As Elizabeth's inner life grows in Carmel, her letters effectively become spiritual guidance. Elizabeth increasingly becomes a "little mother" to all her correspondents and, most poignantly, to her own mother with whom there is a significant and explicit role reversal: "I'm the little mother of your soul";[1] and her younger sister, Guite, becomes "my darling daughter."

Elizabeth is keenly interested in all the concerns of her friends, spiritual and material: illness, bereavement, loss of a baby, expecting a baby, finding a husband. All Elizabeth's correspondents are supported and consoled by her deep affection and fervent prayer.

On her deathbed, Elizabeth's courage in suffering edifies her sisters who witness her increasing communion with God. Her letters reveal that her deep recollection is compatible with continuing care for her loved ones: she dies praying for husbands for the daughters of two of her friends, reassuring them that when she gets to heaven she will "interest" the Blessed Virgin in their cause! Hers is no detached spirituality, but rather one which immerses her in the love of God and love of neighbor. She has, in fact, become "another humanity" in which God has renewed his whole mystery of love.

---

1. See L 273.

Letters to Canon Emilien Isidore Angles

Elizabeth's letters to her lifelong friend and correspondent are of particular interest. When she was only seven, it was to Abbé Angles, the curate of St. Hilary's parish, that Elizabeth first whispered, much to her mother's chagrin, "Canon, I want to be a nun." She confides her deepest anxieties, hopes and feelings to him in response to the needs of her heart and his own promptings: "You asked me to write freely to you, and I obey—besides, I think you understand me." Perhaps he was for her a surrogate father, after the death of her beloved papa in 1887 when she had just turned seven. Although Elizabeth often invited him to visit her in Dijon Carmel, he never managed the trip. The priest intuited the depth of Elizabeth's holiness and assiduously preserved all her letters, sensing that they might prove useful one day.

Two months before she entered Carmel, Elizabeth shares with her trusted canon her deep love for God; her pain at the thought of leaving her mother and her intense desire for heaven, are expressed here for the first time.

"Sometimes I feel so homesick for heaven"

Dear Monsieur,

How good God is! How sweet it is to give ourselves, to abandon ourselves entirely to Him! When He wants something, He knows how to overcome all obstacles, smoothing away all difficulties.

I entrusted all my affairs to Him, I asked Him to speak to my dear mama Himself. He did it so well that I didn't need to say anything. Poor mama! If you could only see how good she is! She leaves everything to the good God, realizing He wants me, and she will allow me to enter Carmel in two months. I have so longed for and awaited this day that I feel as though I were dreaming. But do not imagine that I do not feel the sacrifice. Every time I think of the separation, I offer it to God. Could I offer Him a greater sacrifice than that of such a mother as mine? Ah! He understands; He whose heart is so tender knows well that this is for Him and He sustains and prepares me for this sacrifice!

You know that this Good Master wants me all for Himself. I knew it and felt confident; I was sure that He would take me. Thank the good God for your little Elizabeth; He has given her so much, especially graces known only to Himself, those things which take place in the very depths of the soul. Oh! What love! But He knows very well that I love Him and it seems to me that this word says it all.

To live by love, that is to say to live no longer except with Him, in Him, through Him, is this not already to experience heaven on earth? I want to tell you a secret. If you only knew how sometimes I feel so homesick for heaven; I want so much to be there, near Him. It would make me very happy if He were to take me, even before I entered Carmel, for Carmel in heaven is even better, and I should be a Carmelite just the same in heaven. When I tell Mother prioress how I feel she says I am lazy; but I only want what God wants and if He chooses to leave me on earth for a long time, I am ready to live here for Him.

You must think me rather heartless; I am ashamed of the foolish things I write; but you asked me to write freely to you and I obey—besides, I think you understand me.

I still beg your holy prayers, of which I have special need. Oh! Above all, pray for my darling mama; ask God to take my place in her heart that He may be all in all to her.

(L 55, 19 May 1900)

As a result of long hours spent kneeling in prayer, Elizabeth was unable to attend Mass for some time. This letter shows Elizabeth's love of the Eucharist and her mature understanding and conviction of the absolute reality of God's presence within. The fruit, perhaps, of her growing love for her Carmelite name, "Elizabeth of the Trinity"?

"God in me, me in Him, oh that is my life"

Dear Canon,

For the last ten days I have been suffering with a slight attack of synovitis in my knee. But you cannot imagine how happy I am because I feel it is a token of my Beloved's desire for His little bride to participate in the pain of His divine knees on the road to Calvary. I am deprived of church and Holy Communion, but the good God does not need the Sacrament in order to come to me; I feel I have Him with me just as much. It is there in the depths, in the heaven of my soul that I love to find Him as He never leaves me: God in me, me in Him, oh that is my life.

What a consolation to think that, except that we do not see Him, we possess Him already as the blessed possess Him in heaven; that we are able to keep close to Him, never letting ourselves be distracted from Him. Pray that I may let myself be totally taken by Him and carried away. . . .

Did I ever tell you what my name will be in Carmel: Elizabeth of the Trinity! I think this name indicates my personal vocation; isn't it beautiful? I so love the mystery of the Holy Trinity; it is an abyss in which I lose myself.

Only a month to wait! [before entering Carmel] The last moments are agonizing; poor mama. Pray for her. I entrust her completely to the good God. "Think of Me, and I will think of you," Our Lord said to St. Catherine of Siena. It is so sweet to abandon all to Him in whom we know we can trust.

Goodbye, dear Canon. I send you my photograph; I was thinking of Him while it was being taken, so it will bring Him to you. Pray for me, I have much need of it, I assure you.

(L 62, Friday, 14 June 1901)

Elizabeth's delight in Carmel is evident in the first letter she wrote to Canon Angles, only six weeks after entering Carmel. For one so young, she has a profound relationship with God, which she communicates in

*her writing, illuminating the depths to which we are called: what is
true for her, is true for us.*

"All the treasures of the soul of Christ belong to me,
so that I am infinitely rich"

I thank you with all my heart for your kindness to dear
mama; I am not surprised at what she tells me. You know how
grateful I am to you; not a day passes that I do not pray for
you. I feel that all the treasures of the soul of Christ belong
to me, so that I am infinitely rich; and how overjoyed I am to
draw from this source for all those I love and who have done
good to me.

How good God is! I cannot find words to express the happiness that I experience more each day. Here, there is no longer anything but Him. He is All. He suffices for all. I especially
love the hours of the *great silence*, which is when I write to you.
Picture for yourself Elizabeth in the little cell, of which I am so
fond. It is our tiny sanctuary, for Him and me alone; you can
imagine what happy hours I spend here with my Beloved.

Every Sunday, the Blessed Sacrament is exposed in the
small oratory in the house. When I open the door and contemplate the Divine Prisoner who has made me His captive in
Carmel, it seems as though I have opened the door of heaven!
There, I place before Jesus all those who are in my heart, and
there, near to Him, I find them once more. You see, I often
think of you, and I know too that each morning when you offer
the Holy Sacrifice of the Mass, you remember your little Carmelite, who entrusted her secret to you such a long time ago.
I do not regret the years of waiting: my happiness is so great
now that it had to be paid for. Oh! The good God is so good!

I am glad to live during these days of persecution. May we
become truly holy! Ask for me that holiness for which I long. I
want to love as the saints and martyrs loved.

(L 91, 11 September 1901)

*I am like a little woman in love. And
the more I love him, I become even more little*

Elizabeth writes enthusiastically about her first Lent and Easter in Carmel. She experiences such joy in living her contemplative vocation, in the heart of the church's liturgy and of every moment of life, that Carmel feels like an "anticipated heaven."

"I already live in this heaven because I carry it within me;
one seems so near it in Carmel"

Dear Canon,

How good it is to spend Lent, Holy Week and Easter in Carmel! It is something quite unique. With what joy I sang the Easter "Alleluia," enveloped in the white mantle and dressed in the dear habit which I so longed to wear. It was truly wonderful to spend Holy Thursday near to Him; I would have remained there the whole night but the Master wanted me to rest. But that does not matter, does it? We find Him as much in sleep as in our prayer, since He is in all, everywhere, always, at all times. I returned to the choir at two o'clock in the morning; you can guess how happy I was. More and more I love the grilles that make me the prisoner of His love; how good it is to think that we are both captives, chained to each other. More than that, we are one sole victim, offered to the Father for souls, so that they may be wholly consummated in unity.

Whenever you think of your little Carmelite, thank Him for having chosen such a beautiful part for her: it is an anticipated heaven. The horizon is so beautiful! It is He! . . . Oh! What will it be like above since here below our union is so intimate? You know my homesickness for heaven, it does not diminish; but I already live in this heaven because I carry it within me; one seems so near it in Carmel. Will you come and see me one day and continue, through the grille, the conversations you used to have with your little Elizabeth? Do you remember the first time I told you my secret in St. Hilary's cloister? I have spent such happy times with you, and I ask God to reward you for all the good you have done me. I remember well how happy I was when I could have a brief conversation with you and entrust my great secret to you. I was only a child and yet you never doubted the divine call!

(L 111, April 1902)

Elizabeth wrote this letter to celebrate the first anniversary of entering Carmel. Full of gratitude and joy it conveys her growing love of God.

"I love Him with His own love . . ."

How quickly time passes in Him! A year ago He brought me to this blessed ark, and now, as my Father St. John of the Cross says in his *Canticle*:

> The turtle dove
> Has found its longed-for mate
> Upon the verdant river banks.

Yes! I have found Him whom my soul loves, the One Thing necessary which no one can take from me! Oh how good, how beautiful He is! I want to live in perfect silence and adoration so that I may penetrate ever more deeply into Him; to be so filled with Him that I can give Him, through prayer, to those poor souls who are ignorant of the gift of God.

I know that you pray for me every day at Holy Mass. Oh! Place me in the chalice so that my soul, bathed in the blood of my Christ for which I thirst, may become wholly pure, wholly transparent, so that the Trinity may be reflected in me as in a crystal. The Trinity so loves to contemplate its beauty in a soul; this draws it to give itself even more, to come with greater fullness so as to complete the great mystery of love and unity. Ask God that I may live fully my Carmelite life as a bride of Christ, which presupposes such a profound union! Why has He loved me so much? I feel myself to be so little, so full of misery, but I love Him; that is all I know how to do. I love Him with His own love; it is a double current between "He who is and she who is not."

(L 131, 2 August 1902)

This letter, written six months after Elizabeth's solemn profession, vividly describes her intimate sense of God's indwelling presence on the eve of that great day. Several key themes occur: heaven already beginning on earth; her intense love of God; prayer as a ceaseless heart-to-heart, and Elizabeth's beguiling simplicity.

"I understood that my heaven was beginning on earth: *heaven in faith . . ."*

How many things have happened since my last letter! Holy Church has uttered her *"Veni sponsa Christi,"* "Come, bride of Christ!" She has consecrated me and now all is consummated, or rather, everything is beginning, for profession is only a dawn. Each day my "life as bride" seems more beautiful, more luminous, more enveloped in peace and love.

During the night that preceded the great day, while I was in choir awaiting the Bridegroom, I understood that my heaven was beginning on earth: *heaven in faith*, with suffering and immolation for Him whom I love! I want to love Him so much, to love Him as my seraphic Mother Teresa did, even unto death. This is my whole ambition: to be the prey of love. A life of love is so easy in Carmel! The *Rule* tells us every instant, from morning to evening, what the will of the good God is. How I love the *Rule* which shows me the way in which He wishes me to become holy. I do not know whether I shall have the joy of giving my Bridegroom the testimony of blood, but if I follow the Carmelite observance fully, I shall at last have the satisfaction of *spending* myself for Him, and for Him alone. Then what does it matter how He wishes me to employ myself, since He is always with me? Prayer, the heart-to-heart, must never end. I feel Him so alive in my soul! I have only to recollect myself to find Him within, and this is the source of all my happiness. He has placed in my heart a thirst for the infinite and such a great need for love that He alone can satisfy! I go to Him like a little child to its mother, that He may fill, invade everything; that He may take me and carry me away in His arms. I think we must be so simple with the good God! Will you come some day and give your blessing to your little Carmelite, and join her here in thanking Him for His "exceeding love"? I can no longer describe my joy. Listen to the hymn of my heart for God and for you. Wash me in the blood of the Bridegroom at Holy Mass, for He is the purity of the bride . . . and she is thirsting for it!

(L 169, 15 July 1903)

In this beautiful and moving letter we glimpse Elizabeth's profound experience of God's love. Like many mystics she loses herself in him, expressing herself in words reminiscent of St. Paul's Hymn to Love in 1 Corinthians 13.

"If you only knew how He fills me!"

I remember our conversations during the last holidays we spent together among the beautiful mountains, and how we used to stroll together by moonlight . . . on the hill by the church. How lovely it was in the calm and silence of night! Did you not feel that my whole heart went out to Him? And then Mass in the little chapel, the Mass you said! I shall never forget those happy times. My soul and my heart follow you now, and I feel very near to you.

I delight in the thought of having left all for Him; it is a joy to give when one loves, and I so love this God who is jealous of having me for Himself alone. I feel so much love descending on my soul! It is like an ocean into which I plunge and lose myself; it is my vision on earth while I wait to see Him in the face-to-face vision in light. He is in me and I am in Him. I only have to love and to let myself be loved every moment; to wake in love, to act in love, to sleep in love, my soul in His soul, my heart in His heart, that by His touch He may purify me and free me from my misery. If you only knew how He fills me! I should like to tell you all about it as in the old days at St. Hilary's, and then bathe myself in the precious Blood. I almost commit a sin of envy when I think of dear mama! I beg you, at least, at Holy Mass, to place my soul in the chalice and ask the Bridegroom to make me wholly pure, wholly virginal, wholly one with Him.

(L 177, 27 August 1903)

During Lent, Carmelites traditionally neither wrote nor received letters or had visitors, in order to enter more fully into the "solitude of the desert." This is the "long fast" to which Elizabeth refers. Politically and religiously France was in turmoil as the state "crucified" religious, systematically suppressing all teaching orders, confiscating goods and property, forcing communities to flee the country and regroup in other parts of Europe.

"We really need God to work many
resurrections in our dear France"

Before burying myself in the solitude of the desert, our Reverend Mother has given me leave to let you know how happy your kind letter has made me. Mama told me that you were suffering with your arm, but I hope from what you write that the rheumatism has gone.

Poor mama! She wishes the "Alleluia!" had been sung already. God will reward her motherly heart for its long fast! Yes, Canon, as you say there is so much to expiate and so much to ask for. I believe that if we are to meet so many needs, we must become a living and continual prayer and love much. The power of a soul given wholly to love is indeed great. We see it in Mary Magdalene: one word from her suffices to obtain the resurrection of Lazarus. We really need God to work many resurrections in our dear France; I love to place her under the outpouring of the Divine Blood. St. Paul says that: "In Him we have the forgiveness of sins according to the riches of His grace which He has poured out abundantly on us" (see Eph 1:7–8). This thought does me so much good. Oh! how good it is to go and be consoled by Him during the times when we feel only our miseries, and I am so full of them! But the good God has given me a mother, the image of His mercy, who, with just a word, calms all the anguish of her little one's soul, and gives her wings to fly away beneath the rays of the Creator Star. So, my life is spent in thanksgiving, united to the eternal praise sung by the saints in heaven, while I pass my apprenticeship on earth. . . . Pray for your little child during the holy season of Lent; consecrate her with the sacred Host, so that nothing more may remain of poor Elizabeth, but that she may be wholly "of the Trinity." Then her prayer can become all-powerful, and you will profit by it, since you have such a large share in her prayers, which is only her way of repaying her large debt of gratitude! *A Dieu*, dear Canon, the bell is calling me to Matins [Office of Readings]. I shall not forget to "remember" you; you will be the first. . . .

(L 225, March 1905)

On December 9, 1905, France passed a law separating the Church and State: the rupture was complete. Elizabeth's distress at this dire situation finds expression in this letter, and in a spirit of reparation she immerses herself in prayer and sacrifice.

"Poor France! I love to cover her
with the Blood of the Just One"

How strongly we feel the need to be sanctified, to forget ourselves in order to be totally given to the interests of the Church. Poor France! I love to cover her with the Blood of the Just One, "He who is always living to make intercession for us" (see Heb 7:25). How sublime is the mission of the Carmelite! She must be a mediatrix with Jesus Christ, be another humanity in which He can perpetuate His life of reparation, sacrifice, praise and adoration. Oh! Pray that I may live up to my vocation, that I may not abuse the graces that He showers upon me. How fearful that makes me feel at times! But then I cast myself upon Him whom St. John calls "Faithful and True" (Rev 19:11), and beg Him to be Himself my fidelity!

When I returned to my cell after Mass on Christmas Night, I felt inundated by happiness when remembering past joys, and I said to myself with the Apostle: "For His sake I have suffered the loss of all things" (Phil 3:8)! Ask Him that I may lose myself in order to immerse myself in God. Epiphany Sunday will be the third anniversary of my nuptials with the Lamb, so when you consecrate the host in which Jesus becomes incarnate, will you also consecrate your little child to All-Powerful Love, so that He may transform her into a "Praise of Glory."

(L 256, December 1905)

Elizabeth was too weak to be able to attend Mass and receive Holy Communion. At that time priests were only allowed inside the enclosure to administer Extreme Unction, as the Sacrament of the Sick was then known, therefore Elizabeth received Holy Communion very rarely. In order to bring her some spiritual consolation, Mother Germaine goes straight to Elizabeth's bedside after Mass, in order to "share" her Communion.

"I communicate also within her soul"

I know that I can say anything to you, you who have always been my confidant. My soul is filled with joy at the imminent prospect of gazing on the ineffable beauty of Him whom I love and the thought of immersing myself in the Blessed Trinity. Oh, how much it would cost me to come back to the world which seems so vile to me after my beautiful dream. God alone is perfectly pure and holy; happily, we are able to dwell in Him even in this our earthly exile. However, my Master's pleasure is mine: I surrender myself to Him to do as He wills with me.

Since you are His priest, consecrate me to Him like a little sacrifice of praise who wants to glorify Him in heaven, or on earth with as much suffering as He wishes. And then, if I go, you will help me get out of purgatory. Oh, if you knew how much I feel that everything within me is soiled, everything is miserable: I really need my kind Mother to rid myself of it. She comes to make her thanksgiving [after Communion] every morning beside my little bed, so I communicate also within her soul, and the same love flows in the souls of the mother and her child.

She prays so fervently that I may be cured, that I ask her to let me go and be her guardian angel in heaven. How much I should pray for you there, too; it will be such a delight to me to do something for my dear Canon!

A Dieu; it is so good to await the coming of the Bridegroom. Pray for me that I may be completely surrendered to Him in the suffering He sends me and that I might already live for love alone.

(L 271, 9 May 1906)

One of the most graphic descriptions of Elizabeth's dreadful illness occurs in this, her last letter to her dear Canon.

"If you knew what a work of destruction I feel
throughout my whole being; the road to Calvary has opened"

Your dear letter gave me great joy. Oh, how I love the thought of St. Paul that you sent me. To think it is being realized in me, on this little bed, the altar on which I am being immolated to Love. Oh! Ask that my likeness to the adored Image might become more perfect each day. That is what haunts me, what gives strength to my soul in suffering. If you knew what a work of destruction I feel throughout my whole being; the road to Calvary has opened, and I am wholly joyful to walk it like a bride beside the divine Crucified. I will be twenty-six on the eighteenth of this month and I do not know if this year will end in time or eternity. I ask you again, like a child of her father, to please consecrate me at Holy Mass as a sacrifice of praise to the glory of God. Oh, consecrate me so completely that I may be no longer myself but Him, Jesus! So that the Father on looking at me, may recognize Him. May I be "made conformable to His death" (see Phil 3:10), so that I might suffer in myself what is wanting in His passion for His body, the Church. And then, bathe me in the Blood of Christ so I may be strong with His strength; I feel so little, so weak!

A Dieu, dear Canon Angles, I ask you to bless me in the name of the Holy Trinity, to whom I am especially dedicated. Will you also consecrate me to the Blessed Virgin? It was she, Mary Immaculate, who gave me the habit of Carmel, and I beg her to clothe me with the "robe of fine linen" (see Rev 19:8), in which the bride is dressed to present herself at the marriage feast of the Lamb.

P.S. On August 2, I will have been in religious life for over five years.

(L 294, 8 July 1906)

Letters to Her Mother

Madame Catez would have visited her daughter regularly each month, apart from Advent, Lent, and retreats when there were no visitors. Although she only lived about 650 feet away in an apartment which overlooked the monastery, Elizabeth wrote regularly, ever aware of what her vocation had cost her mother.

Elizabeth's family celebrated feast days more than birthdays, and Elizabeth, sensitive to her mother's feelings and the happy anniversaries they had shared, wrote each year for her mother's feast day, August 15, the Assumption. Elizabeth refers to the agony their separation caused. Notice how she gently draws her mother to deepen her relationship with God, in order to find consolation and share her daughter's happiness.

"The secret of your daughter's happiness . . ."

Do you remember how carefully your Elizabeth used to hide in order to prepare a pretty surprise present for you? I am also making preparations this year, secret plans with my Divine Bridegroom. He opens all His treasures to me and from them I make a divine bouquet, a crown which will shine on your head for all eternity. Your little daughter will rejoice some day in heaven, thinking that she has helped the Divine Master to make it; that she added beautiful rubies to it, blood from your heart and also from her own! . . .

I am writing in our little cell, which is so full of silence and, above all, full of God. Tonight I feel that I must thank you again, for you well know that I would never have left you without your *"Fiat!"* and He wished me to sacrifice you for love of Him. Carmel is like heaven, and we must separate ourselves from all in order to possess Him who is All; but I love you as one loves in heaven, where there will no longer be any separation between us, for He whom I possess within me also dwells in you so we are closely united.

And now, dear mama, I only have time to wish you one thing: that God, who has taken me for Himself, may become more and more the friend to whom you entrust everything. Live in His intimacy as you would live with One who loves you, in a sweet heart-to-heart; that is the secret of your daughter's happiness; your daughter who embraces you with all the love of her Carmelite heart, the heart that is all yours, for it is all His, all the Trinity's.

(L 170, 13 August 1903)

Elizabeth contrasts Guite's happily married state with her own: Guite seems to have gained everything, Elizabeth given up everything; viewed with the eyes of faith, however, Elizabeth has chosen "the better part." Elizabeth encourages her mother to rejoice because she is privileged to have a daughter who is a Carmelite. Madame Catez esteemed St. Teresa, the Carmelite foundress, and introduced Elizabeth to her writings. Ironically, despite loving this great Carmelite, she opposed her daughter's Carmelite vocation for years.

"From a worldly point of view,
I seem to have made nothing but sacrifices"

Marguerite and her husband came to see me and they
seem so happy! I thanked God on their account . . . and then
on my own. From a worldly point of view, I seem to have made
nothing but sacrifices, but nevertheless, my little mama, I have
the better part. In spite of the tears and sadness this imposes
on a mother's heart, you must rejoice in having given God a
Carmelite, because, next to a priest, I see nothing more holy on
earth: a Carmelite, that implies a divinized being! Ask our holy
Mother, St. Teresa, whom you taught me to love when I was a
little girl, that I may become a holy Carmelite and then rejoice
at being loved by this little heart that is given totally to God. If I
love Him, it is you who led me to Him; you prepared me so well
for our first meeting on that great day when we gave ourselves
to one another! Thank you for all you have done! I long to make
Him loved, and to give Him to souls as you have done.

I give my crucifix a kiss so that my Christ may carry it to
you on behalf of His bride, your loving little daughter.

(L 178, Early September 1903)

*Mother Germaine, concerned about Elizabeth's deteriorating health,
relieved her of some duties, hoping that rest and fresh air would restore
her. In this loving letter for her mother's feast, Elizabeth speaks only of
joy and faith in God's love.*

"My happiness increases daily;
it is taking on infinite proportions"

Our good Mother, who watches over your Elizabeth with
a truly maternal heart, insists upon my spending time in the
fresh air, so instead of working in our little cell, I install myself
like a hermit in the most deserted part of our immense garden,
where I spend delightful hours. Nature seems so full of God:
the wind rustling in the tall trees, the little birds singing, the

beautiful blue sky, all speak to me of Him. O mama, I must tell you how my happiness increases daily; it is taking on infinite proportions, like God Himself, yet it is so calm, so sweet. I should like to tell you my *secret*.

In his first epistle, St. Peter says, "Because you believe, you will be filled with unshakable joy" (see 1 Pt 1:8). The Carmelite actually draws all her happiness from this divine source: faith. She believes, as St. John says, "in the love God has for her." She believes that this same love draws Him to earth and into her soul because He, who is called the Truth, has said in the Gospel, "Remain in me and I in you" (see Jn 15:9). In all simplicity, she obeys this most sweet commandment, living in intimacy with the God who dwells within her, who is more present to her than she is to herself. This is not just sentiment or imagination, dearest mama, it is pure faith; and your own faith is so strong that God could say to you those words: "Woman, great is your faith!" (Mt 15:28). Yes, it was *great* when you led your Isaac to sacrifice him on the mountain! The good God has recorded this heroic act of your mother's heart in the great book of life. I think your page will be very full and that you can await the hour of Divine judgment with peaceful confidence.

Dearest mama, it is your feast on Tuesday, and though in Carmel we do not usually write on such occasions, for we must make sacrifices, especially those which touch our hearts, our Reverend Mother has allowed me to make my letter coincide with the date which is so dear to me. You know that I send you my tenderest wishes. Do you remember how much I used to enjoy preparing my surprises for your feast? I have sacrificed all this on the altar of my heart to Him who is a "Spouse of Blood." It would be far from true to say that it has cost me nothing. Sometimes I wonder how I could have left so good a mother, but the more we give to God, the more He gives, as I realize more and more each day. So I wish you a very happy feast! It would make me so happy if, on the feast of her Assumption, the Holy Virgin were to take with her all your cares, past, present, and to come, for you have a lot I know, and your Elizabeth cannot bear to see a shadow pass over your beloved face.

(L 236, 11 August 1905)

In this remarkable letter, Elizabeth reveals the intensity of her longing for heaven, as she expresses her disappointment in not having died. She truly sees death as the gateway to eternity.

"I will confess my deep disappointment in not going to Him"

My dear Mama,

I have never felt so close to you. Your letter brought such comfort to my heart and joy to my soul. I have kissed it as if it were a precious relic, thanking the good God for having given me such an incomparable mother. If I had gone to heaven, how I would have kept near you! I would never have left you and would have made you feel your Elizabeth's presence.

As I know you will understand me, I will confess my deep disappointment in not going to Him whom I love so dearly. Think what a wonderful Easter Day your daughter would have spent in heaven!... But that was selfish of me and now I ask to be cured. I do so in union with you, Guite, and my dear little angels, whom I would have delighted in protecting, had I taken my flight.

If you only knew how kind our Mother is! She is a real mama to your daughter and I assure you that, on the night of my crisis, I needed to hear her voice and feel her hand in mine, in spite of my joy at going to God, for it is a solemn moment and one feels so little and empty handed.

(L 266, 15 April 1906)

In this poignant letter, Elizabeth, who is seriously ill, writes to comfort her mother who is also unwell, urging her to live with God and trust in His love.

"Oh mother! Let us prepare for eternity"

Dear Mama,

Your little invalid wants to speak to you from her heart, that heart so full of tenderness for you.

I know that you are ill, and my kind Mother inside the convent, who is always near me, tells me all about your dear health. You cannot imagine what care she lavishes on me, with all the tenderness and delicacy of a mother's heart. How happy I am in the solitude of my infirmary! My Master is here with me and we live night and day in a sweet heart-to-heart. I appreciate the happiness of being a Carmelite more than ever, and I pray to God for the darling mother who gave me to Him. I have been drawn nearer to heaven since this illness began; I will tell you all about it some day.

Oh mother! Let us prepare for eternity; let us live with Him, for He alone can accompany and help us on this great journey. He is the God of love; we can never understand how dearly He loves us, above all when He sends us trials.

(L 267, 19 April 1906)

The complete trust between mother and daughter leads to their roles being reversed as Elizabeth becomes spiritual mother.

"I am the little mother of your soul"

What a consolation it is to be able to open my soul to my mother and feel that yours is one with mine. I feel as if my love for you is not only that of a child for the best of mothers but also that of a mother for her child. I am the little mother of your soul; that is all right, isn't it? We are going into retreat for Pentecost, I even more so in my dear little cenacle, separated from everyone. I am asking the Holy Spirit to reveal to you the presence of God within you, which I have already spoken to you about. You may believe my doctrine, because it is not mine. If you read St. John's Gospel you will see that the Divine Master constantly insists on this commandment: "Abide in me as I abide in you" (Jn 15:4). And again, "Those who love me will keep my word, and my Father will love them, and we will come to them and make our home with them" (Jn 14:23).

St. John, in his epistles, wants us to have "fellowship" with the Holy Trinity; what a sweet and simple word to use! St. Paul says that it is enough to believe: "God is spirit" (Jn 4:24) and we approach Him through faith. Realize that your soul is the temple of God; it is again St. Paul who says this (1 Cor 3:16–17; 2 Cor 6:16); the three Divine Persons dwell within you at every moment of the day and night. You do not possess the Sacred Humanity as you do when you receive Holy Communion; but the divinity, the essence which the blessed adore in heaven, is in your soul; when you realize that there is a wholly adorable divine intimacy within, you are never alone again!

(L 273, 27 May 1906)

Mysticism begins and ends with the conviction of being loved by God: Elizabeth was a mystic par excellence.

"My life can be summed up in one phrase"

My life can be summed up in one phrase which might be inscribed upon every moment of my time, "for His exceeding charity " (see Eph 2:4). Whatever happens to me is a message or an assurance of the *exceeding love* of God; I cannot live my life apart from that. . . .

(L 280, 12 June 1906)

The triduum referred to honored the sixteen Carmelites of Compiègne, guillotined during the French Revolution and beatified by Pope Pius X on May 27, 1906. Elizabeth's final illness is, in fact, a very real martyrdom. Notice how she reminds her mother to pray during her journey.

> "If I am not a martyr of blood,
> I wish to be a martyr of love"

Your Carmelite's soul will be taking part with your own in the triduum of our blessed Martyrs. Oh, what an honor it would be if your daughter could also offer God the witness of her blood! Then it would be worthwhile to have stayed on earth and seen the dream of Heaven fade away. . . .

. . . What I want of Him most of all is the martyrdom of love which consumed our holy Mother Teresa, and since Truth Himself has declared that the greatest proof of love is to give our life for Him we love, I give Him mine, which has long been His, that He may do as He wills with it. If I am not a martyr of blood, I wish to be a martyr of love. Dear mama, let us love God, and live with Him as with one we love, one from whom we cannot be separated. Tell me if you are becoming more recollected, for I care deeply for your soul. Remember the words of the Gospel: "The Kingdom of God is among you" (Lk 17:21). Enter this little Kingdom to adore the sovereign Monarch who resides there as in His own palace. He loves you so much! He has given you proof of His love, by asking you so often on your path of life, to help Him to carry His cross.

P.S. Remember to pray while you are on the train on Friday, as that is a very good opportunity for prayer.

(L 287, 19 June 1906)

Despite increasing weakness, Elizabeth strives to amuse her mother and alleviate her concerns about her condition.

"Do not cry over your Elizabeth"

My stomach is still recalcitrant, but can you believe that I have started to walk! I cannot understand it, for I am no stronger than before when I could not even sit up.

The other day when our Mother came to see me, I felt so exhausted that I told her I was going. "It would be much better if you tried to walk instead of talking like that," she said. I love to obey her, so when I was on my own I tried to walk by the side of the bed but it hurt me dreadfully. After asking Sister Thérèse of the Child Jesus not to cure me, but to give me the use of my legs, I was able to walk. I am like an old woman doubled up over her cane. Our Mother takes me on her arm onto the terrace. I am quite proud of my comings and goings and I cannot wait to give you a demonstration; I am sure you would laugh, because I look very funny. I am very glad to tell you this good news and know that it will make you very happy.

Do not cry over your Elizabeth; the good God will leave her here with you a little longer, and when she is in heaven she will always be bending over her mother, the mother who is so good and whom she loves more dearly every day. Oh, dearest mother, let us look above! It rests the soul to think that heaven is the Father's house; that He awaits us there as if we were beloved children returning home after a time of exile, and that He makes Himself our traveling companion to lead us there.

(L 295, 11 July 1906)

Elizabeth so identifies with her crucified Bridegroom that she longs to share in his passion.

"A victim of suffering"

You fear that I am destined to be a victim of suffering; I beg of you not to grieve over what would be so beautiful. I feel unworthy of it! Just think what it would mean, to participate in the sufferings of my crucified Bridegroom; to go with Him to my passion; to share in His work of redemption!

(L 300, 18 July 1906)

Recalling her entry into Carmel, Elizabeth comments on the painful separation and also the graces received during her Carmelite life. She longs to share the happiness which comes from living in God's presence, and stresses the importance of waiting patiently on God.

"But they do not know how to wait"

Dearest Mama,

Do you recall this day, five years ago? I remember it well, and He does too! . . . He has collected up the blood from your heart in a chalice which will weigh heavy in the balance of His mercy!

Yesterday, when I was recalling our last evening together and how, because I could not sleep, I settled myself close to the window and stayed there until near midnight, in prayer with my Master, I spent a heavenly evening. The sky was so blue, so calm; one could feel such a silence in the monastery . . . and I thought over these five years so filled with graces. Dearest mama, never regret the joy you have given me. Yes, thanks to your "*Fiat!*" I have been able to enter this holy dwelling and, alone with God the Alone, I have enjoyed a foretaste of that heaven which so attracts my soul.

Tonight I have made a second offering of your sacrifice five years ago, that it may shower blessings upon her whom I love more than anyone. Live with Him. Ah, how I wish I could tell all souls what sources of strength, of peace, and of happiness they will find if they would only consent to live in this intimacy. But they do not know how to wait; if God does not give Himself to them in a perceptible way, they leave His presence, and when He comes to them laden with His gifts He finds no one there; the soul has gone outside itself in external things, and no longer dwells in its inner depths. Recollect yourself from time to time, dear mama, and then you will be very close to your Elizabeth.

(L 302, 2 August 1906)

As Elizabeth's sufferings increased, she accepted them joyfully as a living Mass: her life is the sacrifice, his love is the priest, and her bed is the altar. She reassures her mother of the honor they should feel in being associated with Christ's work of redemption.

"This Mass which He is saying with me, for which
His love is the priest, may last a long time yet"
Jesus.

The good God is pleased to immolate His *hostie* ("little victim"),[2] but this Mass which He is saying with me, for which His love is the priest, may last a long time yet. The little victim does not find the time long in the hands of the Master who is sacrificing her, and she can say, dear mama, that if she passes on the way of suffering, she is following the path of true happiness, which no one can take from her. Your mother's heart should leap for divine joy in thinking that the Master has deigned to choose your daughter, the fruit of your womb, to associate her with His great work of redemption; that He has signed her with the seal of the cross and that He suffers in her, as it were, an extension of His passion. The bride belongs to the Bridegroom; He has taken me for His own. He wants me to be another humanity for Him in which He can suffer still more for the glory of His Father, to help the needs of the Church; this thought has done me so much good! Our Mother often speaks to me of it; I close my eyes and listen, forgetting that it is she, for it seems as though the Master were beside me, encouraging and teaching me how to bear His cross.

This kind Mother, so eloquent about self-sacrifice, thinks of nothing but relieving my pain, as I often remind her. However, I submit to her like a child, remembering that Our Lord

2. In French, the original word "*hostie*" signifies the sacred host at Mass as well as the ordinary victim. The word "victim" or "sacrifice" does not render the full richness of the French.

told St. Teresa that He preferred her obedience to the penances of another saint. So I take Guite's little dainties, when my stomach allows it, and they relieve it more than anything else. . . . I do my best for love of the good God not to starve it to death.

(L 309, September 1906)

Elizabeth first encountered this profound insight into suffering while reading Angela of Foligno's Book of Visions *and* Instructions, *first referring to it in a letter to Guite on the feast of the Exaltation of the Cross, September 14. Elizabeth, like many saints, embraces the cross as a means of intimate union with Christ, crucified by love.*

"Where did He dwell, if not in suffering?"

With each new suffering, I kiss my Master's cross and say to Him: "Thank you, but I am not worthy of it," because I think that suffering was the companion of His life, and I do not deserve to be treated as His Father treated His Son.

In speaking of Jesus, a saint once wrote: "Where did He dwell, if not in suffering?" Every soul that is bruised by suffering of whatever kind, can say to itself, "I dwell with Jesus; we live in intimacy, sheltered within the same dwelling."

The saint of whom I speak teaches us that the sign which proves that God dwells in us and that we are possessed by His love is that we take what hurts us not only patiently, but gratefully, knowing ourselves blessed. In order to reach this state we must profoundly contemplate Christ Crucified by love. If genuine, this contemplation cannot fail to lead us to love suffering.

Dearest mama, regard every trial, every contradiction, in the light that shines from the Cross; then you will be pleasing to God and grow in the ways of love. Oh, thank Him for me! I am so very happy! I wish I could shed a little of this happiness on those I love.

A Dieu! I cannot hold my pencil any longer, but my heart remains with you. I appoint the shadow of the cross as our rendezvous, there to learn the science of suffering.

Your happy daughter . . .

(L 314, September 1906)

Letters to Guite

Elizabeth and her sister Marguerite, known as "Guite," were incredibly close from their earliest years, notwithstanding their different personalities and gifts: whereas Elizabeth had a strong and passionate character, Guite was gentle, shy, and quiet. Although Guite felt she had little understanding of the things of God and Elizabeth's relationship with him, she adored her "big sister." On Palm Sunday March 26, 1889, Guite heroically persuaded their mother to give Elizabeth permission to enter Carmel. Realizing the cost of their separation to her "little sister," Elizabeth wrote often and lovingly to her, sharing her happiness in Carmel and constantly urging Guite to share her joy and spiritual discoveries. Guite credited all her growth in understanding and love of God to Elizabeth, confiding to Father Philipon that Elizabeth taught her about the interior life; she was an apt pupil. Guite's beloved husband, Georges, died suddenly at the age of forty-two, leaving her to raise their nine children. After her death, it was said that Guite was like the wise woman in Scripture who always sacrificed herself for her family and for others.

So effective was Elizabeth's spiritual guidance and Guite's wholehearted response that when news of Elizabeth's cause for canonization was circulated in Dijon, family and friends considered Guite an even worthier candidate! Guite's nine children unanimously testify to their mother's holiness. Incredibly, Guite never spoke to them of Elizabeth, but they felt that she always lived in the company of her beloved sister, always prayerful, recollected, and full of faith. Guite is the first and most convincing witness of the efficacy of Elizabeth's spiritual teaching.

This letter was written barely a month after Elizabeth entered Carmel. Guite has asked for all the details of her new life, and Elizabeth obliges, joyfully describing the practical and spiritual aspects of Carmelite life.

"Everything is delightful in Carmel!"

As you like to hear all the details, I will tell you about something interesting. We've done the wash. For the occasion, I turned up my dress, covered myself entirely with a huge apron, and in order to complete my costume, put on a pair of clogs. I went down to the wash house where everyone was rubbing away with all their might and I tried to do the same. I splashed and soaked myself completely, but never mind, I was thrilled with it all! Oh! you see, everything is delightful in Carmel! We find the good God at the wash just the same as at prayer; there is nothing but Him everywhere. We live Him and breathe Him. If you knew how happy I am! My horizon grows larger each day.

(L 89, August 1901)

Traveling widely with her mother and sister before entering Carmel, Elizabeth enjoyed the beautiful scenery and vast horizons. Countering the view that an enclosed life is limiting, she wrote of the limitless spiritual horizons of a life lived so close to the God of Love. This is the first time that Elizabeth refers to her life in Carmel as an anticipated heaven; it becomes a recurring theme.

"Carmel . . . is an anticipated heaven"

My dear Guite,

I address my letter to Luneville, as I think you are there now. I entrust you with lots of affectionate messages for Mademoiselle Adelin. Tell her that the grille of Carmel, which made her blood freeze and seemed so somber to her, looks golden to me. Ah! if we could only raise the curtain, what a beautiful horizon we should see on the other side, it is infinite! And that

is why it grows each day. Carmel, which is being alone with
Him whom we love, is an anticipated heaven. Do not be jealous. He alone knows what a sacrifice I made in leaving you. I
know that I could never have done it if His love had not sus-
tained me, for I love you so much, and it seems to me that this
love grows each day for He divinizes it.

These carnival days are delightful and full of God.[3] The
Blessed Sacrament is exposed and I spend as much of the day
as I can near Him and you, Guite, are there with me, because
you are always in my soul. We are in the dark because the
grille is open, and all the light comes from Him. I like to see
this great grille between us. He is a prisoner for me and I am a
prisoner for Him.

Since mama is interested in news of my health, tell her
that I am quite well. I would not even notice it was winter if
it were not for the pretty curtains with which the good God
covers the windows. How charming the cloister looks with its
frosted panes!

Live close to God; we are one in Him.

(L 109, 16 February 1902)

*This extract, written on the first feast of the Holy Trinity Elizabeth
celebrated in Carmel, echoes an important insight she had shared with
Canon Angles before entering.*

"The vocation hidden in my name"

. . . This is my own feast; there is no other like it for me.
It is celebrated in silence and adoration in Carmel. I never
before realized the full meaning of the vocation hidden in my
name. Let this great mystery be our rendezvous, our center,
our dwelling.

(L 113, 25 May 1902)

_____

3. Monday and Shrove Tuesday, before Ash Wednesday, celebrated in Europe.

In sharing Guite's joy, Elizabeth enfolds her and the baby in prayer, suggesting that Guite open herself totally to God, so that her child will enter the world suffused with his presence. A profound insight, anticipating later psychological understanding.

"How I enfold you in prayer"

"The Kingdom of God is among you" (Lk 17:21).

Dear Guite,

What pleasure you gave me on my feast by your kind message and your lovely photograph! St. Elizabeth must have inspired you because it was just what I wanted. It helps me to become recollected, and then it seems as if we two were both close to our Lord. It is really true that He is in our souls and that we are always near Him, like Martha and Mary. While you are busy, I keep you close to Him. You know that, when we love, external things cannot distract us, and Guite is Martha and Mary at the same time!

How I enfold you in prayer, you and the dear little creature that is already in the mind of God! Let yourself be given up to and possessed by His Divine life, so that the little one will enter this world enriched with blessings.

I hope you have a beautiful baby and I am delighted to think what happiness it will bring with it. I thank God and I share your joy from the depth of my beloved solitude.

(L 183, 22 November 1903)

On the birth of Guite's baby, which she and Georges named for her aunt, Elizabeth expresses the depth of her theological understanding of the dignity conferred by the sacrament of baptism.

"I feel full of reverence before this little temple
of the Blessed Trinity"

I feel full of reverence before this little temple of the Blessed Trinity; her soul seems to me like a crystal which

radiates God. If I were near her, I would kneel down to adore
IIim who dwells within her. . . . How I should like to cradle
her in my arms! But the good God has called me to the mountain so that I can be her angel and envelop her in prayer, and I
joyfully sacrifice all the rest to Him for her sake. How happy I
feel to think that you are a mother! I confide you and your little angel to the care of Him who is love itself. I adore Him with
you and embrace you in His heart.

(L 197, 12 March 1904)

*Writing for her sister's feast, Elizabeth plays on the Latin meaning of
Marguerite, daisy, an idea she has already used figuratively in two poems.*

"Echo of my soul "

"The eye of God is upon her, His love surrounds her like a rampart."

(see Ps 31:21–22)

Dear Little Sister,
    "Echo of my soul," as Sister Thérèse of the Child Jesus
called one of her sisters. I love to give you this sweet name on
the eve of your feast.
    My darling flower, my Marguerite, I beg God to grant all
the wishes of your big "heart of gold," to send down on you
the fire of His love, that beneath these divine rays you may
grow and bloom, and that in the shadow of your "great white
petals," another little flower very dear to my heart may open
its tender bud.
    How pretty your little Sabeth is! She made me all sorts of
charming little signs yesterday, from the arms of her delighted
grandmother. She looked so sweet with her eyes closed and
her hands crossed over her heart. I made Reverend Mother
smile when I told her that my niece was an "adorer"; that is
her vocation as a "House of God."

(L 204, 19 July 1904)

Elizabeth deepens her relationship with Guite, whom she constantly encourages to live a life of close union with God.

"Let us dwell in the heaven of our soul"

"God is Love" (1 Jn 4:16).

My darling little sister,

Yes, I do indeed find you at the feet of Jesus; and I never leave you, but share the joy of His Heart at finding a *Marguerite* wherein He can rest. Be His paradise in this land where He is so little known and loved; open your heart wide and welcome Him as your guest, and there in the little cell of your soul, love Him, Marguerite! He thirsts for love: keep Him company. . . . I am pleased with you, and the Master loves His little blossom.

It seems a long time since we climbed the mountains together; I remember what a lovely view we had from our room. Don't you find that nature speaks to you of God? The soul needs silence in order to adore Him. Enjoy beautiful Switzerland and our dear mother's companionship. I can understand that you are making a sacrifice in going so far from Georges. It is the law of this life: sacrifice and joy go side by side. The good God wishes to remind us that we have not yet reached our final happiness. Still we are going in that direction and He Himself will carry us in His arms. There in heaven, little sister, He will satisfy all our longings. Meanwhile let us dwell in the heaven of our soul, where we can already be so happy.

(L 210, 21 August 1904)

This letter, written over several days, contains many of Elizabeth's favorite themes and Scripture passages, including: Eph 1:4–6 and Rom 8:17. She reiterates her central message, from 1 Jn 4:16: "Always believe in God's love." Elizabeth encourages Guite, a mother of two little girls, to make a month's retreat, in the midst of her motherly cares, urging her to enter within, living as a contemplative in the world. Elizabeth

used Guite's experience of motherhood as a way into understanding the
mystery of God's love so eloquently expressed by St. Paul.

"I have so many things to say to my Guite!"

"But anyone united to the Lord becomes one spirit with him."

(1 Cor 4:17)

My Dear Little Sister,

Today is Sunday, the happiest of days, for I spend it before the Blessed Sacrament exposed in the oratory, except for the time when I am at the turn. I take advantage of that time to have a chat with you, beneath the eyes of Him we love. I have chosen a large sheet of paper because I have so many things to say to my "Guite"!

Lately I have been reading some splendid things in St. Paul about the mystery of divine adoption and, naturally, I thought of you. Being a mother, you know what depth of love for your children God has put into your heart, so you can grasp the great mystery of our being children of God. Doesn't it thrill you? Listen to what St. Paul says: "Just as he chose us in Christ before the foundation of the world . . . He destined us for adoption as His children . . . to the praise of His glorious grace . . ." (Eph 1:4–6 *passim*). Almighty as He is, it does not seem to me as if He could have done anything greater. Again, "And if children, then heirs" (Rom 8:17). And what is this inheritance? . . .

O Guite! This heaven is the center of our soul; as St. John of the Cross says, when we are in its deepest center, we are in God. How simple and consoling it is! In the midst of your motherly cares and occupations you can withdraw into this solitude and give yourself up to the Holy Spirit. He may thus transform you into God, impressing the divine image of His beauty on your soul, in order that, when the Father looks down on you, He may see nothing but His Christ, and may say: "This is my beloved daughter in whom I am well pleased!"

 our BVM

Little sister, I shall rejoice in heaven at seeing the beauty of my Christ shining in your soul. I shall not be jealous, but shall say to Him, with a mother's pride: It is I, wretched creature as I am who brought forth your life into this soul (see 1 Cor 4:15). St. Paul spoke in this way to his followers and I want to imitate him. What do you think?

Meanwhile, like St. John, let us "believe in His love" (1 Jn 4:16), that love with which God loves us. Since we possess Him within us, what does it matter if our heaven is obscured by night? If Jesus seems to sleep, let us rest beside Him; let us be calm and silent; do not let us wake Him, but wait in faith. I do not think that while Sabeth and Odette are in their mother's arms they trouble themselves much as to whether there is sunshine or rain; let us imitate the little ones and rest in the arms of God with the same simplicity.

I was always fond of a large park, for solitude is a delight. I think you appreciate it too. Will you make a retreat with me for a month ending on September 14? Our Mother has given me this little holiday from the turn so that I shall not have to talk or think about it; I am going to bury myself in the depths of my soul, that is, in God. Will you imitate me in this very simple movement?

When your many duties distract your attention, I shall try to compensate for you, and you, if you like, will enter each hour into the center of your soul where your Divine Guest dwells. You might like to think of those beautiful words I quoted to you: "Do you not know that you are God's temple and that God's Spirit dwells in you?" (1 Cor 3:16) and those of the Master: "Abide in me, as I abide in you" (Jn 15:4). They say that St. Catherine of Siena always dwelt in her cell even when in the midst of the world, for she lived in that inner dwelling place in which my Guite, too, knows how to live. . . .

(L 239, 13 August 1905)

Elizabeth was reluctant to share her feelings with her mother, for fear of distressing her. However, convinced that she was dying, Elizabeth wrote unreservedly to Guite, leaving what she thought would be a "Last Testament." It must have been a very moving letter to read, as Guite later testified that they did not think they would see each other again.

"Little sister, I shall rejoice to go to heaven to be your angel there"

I do not know whether the hour has come for me to pass from this world to my Father, for I am much better and the little saint of Beaune seems to want to cure me. Yet, at times, it seems as if the Divine Eagle were about to swoop down upon His little prey and carry it off to where He lives in the realms of dazzling light.

You have always forgotten your own interests where your Sabeth's happiness was concerned, and I am sure that if I go, you will rejoice at the thought of my first meeting with Divine Beauty. When the veil falls, how happy I shall be to pass into Him, into the very secret of His Face. There I shall spend my eternity in the bosom of the Trinity which is already my dwelling place here below. our Heaven starts here already

Just think, Guite, what it will be to contemplate the splendor of the Divine Being in His own light; to penetrate into the manifold depths of His mystery; to be one with Him we love; to sing unceasingly of His glory and His love; to "be like Him, because we shall see Him as He is!" (see 1 Jn 3:2).

Little sister, I shall rejoice to go to heaven to be your angel there, and I shall be zealous for the beauty of your soul that I have loved so dearly even here on earth!

I leave you my devotion to "the Three." Live within, with Them, in the heaven of your soul; the Father will overshadow you, placing something like a cloud between you and the things of this earth in order to keep you all His. He will communicate His power to you so that you can love Him with a love as strong as death. The Word will imprint in your soul, as in a crystal, the image of His own beauty, so you may be pure with His purity, luminous with His light. The Holy Spirit will transform you into a mystical lyre, which, in silence, beneath His divine touch, will produce a magnificent canticle to Love; then you will be "the praise of His glory" I dreamed of being on earth. You will take my place. I will be *"Laudem Gloriae"* before the throne of the Lamb, and you will be *"Laudem Gloriae"* in the center of your soul; we will thus be united for all eternity.

Always believe in love. If you have to suffer think that it is because you are even more loved; love and always sing in thanksgiving.

Teach the little ones to live under the gaze of God: I should like Elizabeth to have my devotion to the Holy Trinity. I shall be present at their First Holy Communion, and I will help you to prepare them for it.

You must pray for me. I have offended my Master more than you think; but above all, thank Him, and say a *Gloria* every day. Forgive me for the bad example I have often given you.

A Dieu! How I love you! Perhaps I shall soon be lost in the furnace of love. What does it matter? Whether we are in heaven or on earth, we only want to live in love and to glorify Love.

(L 269, April 1906)

At the beginning of July, Elizabeth again felt she was dying. This encouraging letter, contains familiar themes and must have been particularly precious to Guite who, her children tell us, treasured all Elizabeth's letters, constantly rereading them. If Guite ever left Dijon, she entrusted Elizabeth's letters and the statue of Our Lady which Elizabeth had named "Janua Caeli," to the prioress of Carmel, collecting them immediately on her return.

"Believe in this love always, especially in your saddest times"

Dear little sister,

You must erase the word "discouragement" from your dictionary of love. The more you feel your weakness and experience difficulty in recollecting yourself, and the more Our Lord seems hidden, the more you must rejoice, for then you are truly giving to Him, and when we love is it not better to give than to receive? God said to St. Paul: "My grace is sufficient for you for power is made perfect in weakness" (2 Cor 12:9). The great saint understood this so well, for he says: "So, I will boast all the more gladly of my weaknesses, so that the power of Christ may dwell in me" (ibid.).

What does it matter what we feel? He, He is the Immutable One; He is the one who never changes. He loves you today as He loved you yesterday and as He will love you tomorrow. Even if you have grieved Him, remember that abyss calls to another abyss (see Ps 42:7) and that the abyss of your misery attracts the abyss of His mercy. God has made me understand this truth, and it is for both of us. He has also drawn me strongly to suffering and to the gift of self; is this not the whole point of love! Let us lose no opportunity for sacrifice; there are so many we can make throughout the day. You have many opportunities with your babies. Oh! give them all to the good Master! Do you not find that suffering binds you more closely to Him? So, if He takes away your sister, it will be to give Himself even more to you. Help me to prepare for eternity: I do not think my life will last much longer. You love me enough to rejoice that I am going to rest where I have already lived for a long time. I like to tell you these things, "little echo of my soul." I am selfish for, perhaps, I am going to hurt you, but I want to lift you above all that can die . . . into the bosom of Infinite Love. That is the homeland of the two little sisters; there they will meet and part no more.

Oh, Guite! As I write to you this evening my heart is overflowing, for I feel the "exceeding love" of My Master and I wish I could make my soul pass into yours so you could believe in this love always, especially in your saddest times. When you wake in the night, unite yourself to your Sabeth. I wish I could invite you here near me; it is so mysterious and silent, this little cell with its white walls that set off a black wooden cross without a *corpus*. It is mine, the place where I must immolate myself at every moment in order to be conformed to my crucified Bridegroom. I am the good God's little recluse. I love solitude with the Alone, and lead a delightful hermit's life. I, too, am often incapable of doing what I wish and need to seek my Master who keeps Himself well hidden. Then I revive my faith and I am content to relinquish the joy of His presence to give Him the joy of my love.

I have been thinking about the feast of St. Margaret for a while now and I think I can give you something better than anyone else because I am not offering you anything perishable, but what is divine and eternal. I am preparing for the day through a great novena. Every morning I say *Sext* for you, which is the hour consecrated to the Word, so that He may stamp His likeness in your soul that you may be another Christ. Then I offer *None* for you, which I dedicate to the Father, that He may possess you like a beloved daughter, that with "strong hand and an outstretched arm" (Ps 136:12) He may lead you in all your ways, and may turn your steps more fully toward that abyss where He dwells, and in which He wishes you to hide away in Him.

A Dieu! May the "Three" bless my three little *offerings*, and make their heaven and place of rest within each of them! O Abyss! O Love! This is our refrain on our lyres as being the praises of glory, and that is how I shall end this letter.

St. Paul said, "What I want is to know him, Christ, to share his sufferings, so as to become like Him in His death." By this is understood that mystical death by which the soul annihilates itself; and forgets itself so completely that it goes to die in God in order to be transformed in Him.

(L 298, 16 July 1906)

Letter to Sabeth and Odette

This letter, which Elizabeth's two nieces would only have read years later, echoes the sublime insights of L 197, above. Sabeth, Elizabeth's eldest niece, also entered Dijon Carmel, as Sister Elizabeth of Jesus. Odette, in her older sister's words was "a better eldest child than I." Her siblings felt they owed Odette a great deal as she sacrificed her own desire for a husband and family, in order to help their mother after the father's premature death.

"The eyes of faith see in you
a nature of infinite grandeur"

My dear little nieces, my two beautiful, pure, white lilies, whose calyxes contain Jesus. If you knew how I pray to Him for you, that He may overshadow you and protect you from all harm (see Ps 91:4, 10).

To those who contemplate you in your mama's arms, you seem very small, but your fond aunt who looks on you with the eyes of faith sees in you a nature of infinite grandeur, because from all eternity you were in the mind of God. He "predestined you to be conformed to the image of His Son Jesus" (see Rom 8:29) and by holy Baptism He has clothed you with Himself, thus making you His children, and at the same time His "living temple" (see 2 Cor 6:16).

O dear little sanctuaries of love, when I see the splendor that radiates in you, and yet which is only the dawn, I fall silent and adore Him who creates such marvels!

(L 240, August 1905)

Letters to Françoise de Sourdon

Nowadays we would describe Françoise as a "handful": she was a will-ful, temperamental, difficult child who, nonetheless wanted to love God. Aged only fourteen, she was devastated to learn that Elizabeth, who had been her friend and mentor for years, was to enter Carmel. Elizabeth's letters to "Framboise" [Raspberry], her pet name from a play on Françoise, both before and after entering, demonstrate a combi-nation of deep affection, straight talking, and firm guidance. One can see why the community fostered hopes of Elizabeth as a potential leader. Her letters to Françoise are also valuable in giving us a possible insight into how Elizabeth handled her own character.

Is Elizabeth revealing here, perhaps, her "strategy" for dealing with her own tempestuous nature? She overcame self-love by loving God without counting the cost, and she offers a very practical model for young people in dealing with difficulties both within and without: turn to God and he will gradually bring peace.

"As your nature is like mine, I know what you can do"

My dear little Françoise,

I see that my little Framboise is no nearer being converted, and I assure you that this grieves me. I overlooked your fits of temper in the past, but now that you are no longer a baby, such scenes are ridiculous. I know that you will allow your Elizabeth to say anything to you, so I shall speak my mind; you must absolutely set to work on this. As your nature is like mine, I know what you can do. If you only knew what it is to love God and to give Him all He asks, especially when it costs, you would not be slow in heeding my advice. No doubt, you would feel the sacrifice at first, but later you would enjoy such a delightful peace. I want you to be so good! As I am not there for you to pour out all your feelings to, I'm going to suggest something to you. Whenever you wish to confide in me, run to your room and recollect yourself for a moment between your

crucifix and my portrait, which you love so much, and imagine
that I am there with Jesus and my little Framboise. Whenever
you feel out of sorts, will you do that for me?
Thank God for me, I am so happy! You do not understand
it. . . . If you only knew how sweet it is to love Him solely! I
beg Him with all my heart to help you to understand that.

(L 98, October/November 1901)

*It is important to remember that Françoise was only fifteen when
Elizabeth wrote this direct and challenging letter. She advises her to
build a little cell within her soul, finding in God's presence rest, relaxation, and happiness. There, too, she will encounter Elizabeth.*

"If only I could teach you the secret
of happiness as God has taught me!"

Yes, I pray for you and I keep you in my soul close to the
good God, in that little inner sanctuary where I find Him at
all hours of the day and night. I am never alone: my Christ is
always there praying within me, and I pray with Him.

You grieve me, for I sense how unhappy you are, and I
assure you that it is your own fault. If only I could teach you
the secret of happiness as God has taught me! You say that I
have neither cares nor sufferings. It is true that I am happy, but
in the way one can be even while one is being contradicted.
We must fix our gaze on God. It requires an effort at first when
we are boiling with anger, but gently and with patience and
the help of grace, we win through in the end. Build a little cell
within your soul as I do. Remember that the good God is there,
and enter it from time to time. When you feel anxious or
unhappy, seek refuge there at once and confide everything to
the Divine Master. If you got to know Him even a little, prayer
would not weary you any more.

You used to love to come and sit close beside me and tell
me all your secrets: that is how you ought to go to Him. If only

you understood that you would not suffer any more. That is the secret of life in Carmel.

I keep you in the little cell of my soul as you must keep me in yours; then we shall never be apart.

(L 123, 19 June 1902)

Elizabeth astutely uses her friendship to persuade Françoise to be submissive both to her parents and God, affectionately calling her "my own little child."

"I understand your craving for an ideal"

I still have the long letter you wrote to me before you left. I have read it again and again, begging the divine Ideal to captivate and wound the dear little heart He seeks and surrounds as it struggles to escape Him, and live engrossed in things immeasurably below the end for which He created it and placed it in this world!

I understand your craving for an ideal, that is, something to draw you out of yourself and raise you to a higher plane; but the ideal is to be found in Him alone: the only Truth. If you did but know Him in even the smallest degree, as your Sabeth knows Him! . . . He fascinates the soul: beneath His gaze the horizon becomes vast, beautiful, and luminous. I love Him passionately, and in Him I find my all. It is through Him, by His light, that I view all things and perform every action. Will you turn with me toward this sublime Ideal? This is no fiction, but a reality; it is my life in Carmel. Look at Mary Magdalene and see how she was captivated! Since you need to live above yourself, live in Him; it is so simple. And then you must be a consolation to your dear mother. You do not know what there is in the heart of mothers such as God has given you and me. Remember, there is nothing more precious in this world, and I do not think my Master could have asked more from me than to give Him mine. I want you to be perfectly submissive, to dwell in God and in His peace. The more you misbehave, the more intent I am on winning your soul, for the Master wants it. In a way, you are like my own little child and I feel a certain responsibility for you, so do not make your conversion too difficult. Let the Master take you in His nets, it is so good to be there!

(L 128, July 1902)

During their visits, and in letters, Elizabeth counseled Françoise to use her passionate heart to love God. One can almost see what Elizabeth might have been had she not done exactly as she advises Françoise.

"Give Him His proper place in your life"

I have had a very good Lent. Of everything I have seen in Carmel, nothing is more beautiful than Holy Week and Easter Day; indeed, I would say they are quite unique. I will tell you all about them when I see you.

What a joy it is to live in intimacy with God, to spend our life in a heart-to-heart with Him, in a constant exchange of love with the Divine Master, when we know how to find Him in the depths of our soul. Henceforth we are never alone and we long for solitude so that we may enjoy the company of the Guest whom we adore. You must give Him His proper place in your life, in the loving and passionate heart He has given you. If you only knew how good He is, how He is all Love!

I am begging Him to reveal Himself to your soul, to be the friend that you can always find; then you will see all things in a different light and your life would become a joy. This is not meant to be a sermon; rather it is the outpouring of my soul into your own, so that together we may lose ourselves in Him who loves us, as St. Paul says, with an "exceeding love!"

(L 161, 28 April 1903)

Elizabeth's enthusiasm suggests that Françoise is following her advice and surrendering herself to God and allowing him to work in her.

"I feel that God is working in you"

What a beautiful dream I have just had! As I do not have any secrets from you, I think you will understand me when I say it cost me to return to earth. Heaven would only have made the union of our souls even truer. You have often told me that I am like a little mother to you and my heart does feel a maternal affection for you; just think, then, what it would be like if I were in the great Furnace of Love! What divine days I have spent, awaiting the great vision of God! It seemed to me as though a divine Eagle were going to swoop down and carry me off into His dazzling clarity and you can guess the joy I felt in my soul at the thought of seeing the Divine Beauty face-to-face, for the first time. Oh! if I had gone and lost myself in it, how I would have watched over you! I am so ambitious for your soul that I am pleased to suffer in order to draw down superabundant grace on you. Your letter made me immensely happy. I feel that God is working in you and that you are growing closer to Him; that brings me unspeakable joy. It is so good to belong to Him. In the solitude of the infirmary, we are happy, so happy, we two; it is a heart-to-heart which lasts day and night; it is delightful!

A Dieu! I am better and I am sure I will see you again here on earth; in any case, whether in heaven or on earth, our souls are always one.

end of June 18.

(L 270, April 1906)

The Greatness of Our Vocation *July 2018*

This title was later given to Elizabeth's last letter to Françoise de Sourdon, written in pencil because she was too weak to use a pen. Elizabeth attempts to answer the many questions posed by her volatile friend who is distraught at the thought of Elizabeth's imminent death.

Anticipating the great teaching of Lumen Gentium *on the universal call to holiness, Elizabeth once wrote to Madame de Sourdon that the holiness of life, which she enjoyed in Carmel, is the call of "every baptized soul."*[4] *In this letter, Elizabeth develops the idea and counsels an "everyday mysticism" so that through prayer and faith, everything will be "like a sacrament."*[5] *This is one of Elizabeth's most encouraging insights because it speaks to each person's particular way of life: "nothing can be trivial, however commonplace, in itself, for we do not live in, but above such things. . . . Then the soul is truly great, truly free, for our will is enclosed in the will of God."*

Look at every suffering and every joy as coming directly from Him, and then your life will be a continual Communion, since everything will be like a sacrament that will give you God. This is very real, because God is not divided; His will is His whole being. He is wholly and entirely in all things and these things are, to a certain extent, nothing but an emanation of His love! (L 264)

This mini-treatise on the spiritual life has echoes of Jean-Pierre de Caussade and Francis de Sales, Elizabeth's spiritual forebears. Addressed to a young lay woman with a difficult temperament, yet a longing for God, this long letter, a last testament, is full of practical and challenging spiritual advice which could be particularly relevant to today's Christians.

At last, Elizabeth has settled down with her pencil to be near her little Framboise; I say "with her pencil" for have we not been together, heart-to-heart, for a long time? How I love these evening meetings, which are like a prelude to that communion between our souls which will be established when I am in heaven and you on earth. It seems to me that I am like a mother bending over her favorite child. I raise my eyes and look at God, and then I lower them on you, exposing you to the rays of His love. I do not say a word to Him, but He fully understands and prefers my silence. My dearest child, I should

---

4. See *Lumen Gentium*, 40.
5. L 264.

like to be a saint in order to help you here below until I can do it from heaven. What I would not endure for you in order to obtain the graces of fortitude of which you have such need. Now I want to answer your questions. Let us start with humility. I have read splendid passages on this subject. A devout author writes, "The humble soul finds its keenest joy in feeling its powerlessness before God." Dear little friend, pride is not something which is destroyed with one good blow of a sword. No doubt certain heroic acts of humility, like those we read about in the lives of the saints, while not killing it outright, weaken it considerably; but we have to make it die each day. "I die every day," cried St. Paul (1 Cor 15:31). This doctrine of dying to self is the law for every Christian, for Christ said: "If any want to become my followers, let them deny themselves and take up their cross daily and follow me" (Lk 9:23). This doctrine, which seems so austere, takes on a delightful sweetness when we consider that the aim of this death to self is to replace our life of sins and miseries with the life of God. That is what St. Paul meant when he wrote: "Strip off the old man and clothe yourself anew, according to the image of Him who created you" (see Col 3:9–10). This image is God Himself. Recall His will, which He expressed so clearly on the day of creation: "Let us make humankind in our image, according to our likeness" (Gn 1:26).

If we only thought more seriously about our origins, then the things of this world would seem so petty that we would despise them. St. Peter writes, in one of his epistles, that we "may become participants of the divine nature" (2 Pt 1:4). The soul that realizes its own grandeur enjoys "the freedom of the glory of the children of God" (Rom 8:21); that is, it transcends all things, including self. If I were asked the secret of happiness, I should say self-forgetfulness and continual self-d̄ᵉⁿ·¯¯ which effectively destroys pride. The love of
strong enough to destroy all love of self.

Augustine says that we have two cities within us—the city of God and the city of *self*. To the extent that the first increases, the second will be destroyed. A soul that lives by faith, in the presence of God, which has the "single eye" of which Christ speaks in the Gospel, that is the purity of intention which seeks only God; this soul would also live in humility. She would recognize the gifts God had given her, for humility is truth, but would appropriate nothing to itself, attributing everything to God, as the Blessed Virgin did.

All the movements of pride that you feel within you only become faults when your will consents to them. They may cause you great suffering, but they do not offend the good God. These faults, which you commit without thinking, no doubt denote self-love, but that, my dear little friend, is part of our human nature. What God asks of you is that you never willfully dwell on proud thoughts, and never do anything which is motivated by pride, for that would be wrong. But if you find you have done such a thing, do not let yourself become discouraged, because this only comes from irritated pride, but like Magdalene, at the feet of the Master, pour out your miseries before Him, asking Him to set you free from them.

He loves to see a soul recognize its own helplessness; then, as a great saint said: "The abyss of God's immensity encounters the abyss of the creature's nothingness, and God embraces this nothingness."[6]

I have a profound compassion for those who live for nothing higher than this world and its trivialities; I think that they are slaves and I wish I could tell them: "Shake off the yoke that weighs you down. What are you doing, wearing fetters that chain you to yourself and to things less than self?" The happy people in this world are those who have enough contempt and forgetfulness of self to choose the cross for their lot.

---

6. Angela of Foligno.

What delightful peace we experience when we know how to place our joy in suffering!

Have you ever seen those pictures representing death reaping the harvest with his sickle? Well, that is my condition; I seem to feel him destroying me. It is painful for nature, and I assure you that if I remained on that level, I would feel only my cowardice in my suffering. But this is only the human way of looking at it, and I quickly "open the eyes of my soul to the light of faith," which tells me that it is Love who is destroying me and slowly consuming me; then I feel an immense joy and I surrender myself to Him as His prey.

In order to attain the ideal life of the soul, I believe that we must live on the supernatural level. We must be aware that God dwells in the depths of us and we must do all things with Him, then nothing is commonplace even when we are performing the most ordinary tasks, because we do not live in these things, we go beyond them. A supernatural soul never deals with secondary causes, but with God alone. Oh, how its life is simplified! How it resembles the lives of the blessed; how this soul is freed from itself in all things! Everything is reduced to a unity, to that "one thing necessary" (see Lk 10:42) of which the Master spoke to Magdalene. Then the soul is truly great, truly free, because it has "enclosed its will in God's will," as a mystical writer puts it.

When we meditate on our eternal predestination, visible things seem contemptible! Listen to what St. Paul says, "Those whom He foreknew He also predestined to be conformed to the image of His Son" (Rom 8:29). That is not all; you will see, my little one, that you are among the number of the predestined. "And those whom He predestined He has called" (Rom 8:30). It is baptism which has made you a child of adoption, which has stamped you with the seal of the Holy Trinity! "And those whom He called, He also justified" (ibid.). How often have you been justified by the sacrament of penance and by all those touches of God in your soul, without your even being aware of it? "And those whom He justified, He also glorified" (ibid.). This is what awaits you in eternity; but remember that our degree of glory will be the degree of grace in which God finds us at the moment of death. Allow Him to complete His work of predestination in you, and listen to St. Paul again, he will give you a rule of life. Walk in Jesus Christ, "rooted and built up in Him" (Col 2:6–7).

Yes, little child of my soul, walk in Jesus Christ; you need this broad way; you are not made for the narrow paths of this world. Be "rooted in Him," which means being uprooted from yourself, or acting as if you were, by denying yourself at every opportunity. Be "built up in Him," far above all that is passing, where all is pure, all is luminous. "Be established in the faith," that is, never do anything according to your own impressions or imagination, but only according to the great light of God. Believe that He loves you; that He wants to help you in all the struggles you have to undergo; believe in His love, in His "exceeding charity." Nourish your soul on the great truths of the faith which reveal to us how rich we are and the end for which God has created us. If you live in these realities, your devotion will be true. He "loved me and gave Himself for me" (Gal 2:20). That, dear little friend, is the truth!

Finally, grow in gratitude; this is the last word of the program and a natural consequence of all the rest. If you walk "rooted in Jesus Christ, established in faith," your life will be full of gratitude in the charity of the children of God. I wonder how the soul which has fathomed the depths of the love of God's Heart for it can be anything but joyful, whatever suffering and sorrow.

I also wonder what our Reverend Mother will think of this *journal.* She will not let me write hardly at all now, because I am so extremely weak and constantly feel faint. This will probably be the last letter from your Elizabeth; it has taken me days to write, which will explain its incoherence. And yet, this evening, I cannot bring myself to leave you. I am in solitude; it is seven thirty, the community is at recreation, and I feel as if I were already almost in heaven, in this little cell, alone with Him alone, carrying my cross with my Beloved Master; my happiness increases along with my sufferings. If you only knew how to savor the sweetness that lies at the bottom of the chalice prepared by our Father in heaven!

A Dieu, my little one! May He "protect you beneath the shadow of His wings. May He guard you from all evil" (see Ps 91:9).

(L 310, September 1906)

Letters to Germaine de Gemeaux

The Catez "trio," Madame Catez, Sabeth, and Guite were popular guests at the de Gemeaux family chateau. Germaine, like Françoise, was fourteen when Elizabeth entered Carmel. Germaine wanted to become a Carmelite but her mother opposed the idea. Germaine eventually entered the Monastery of the Visitation, Dijon, in 1910.

These letters are of particular interest as Elizabeth is encouraging Germaine to be faithful in responding to God's call to Carmel and they focus explicitly on Elizabeth's growing understanding of her Carmelite vocation, especially her love of the writings of St. John of the Cross.

The first of Elizabeth's letters to Germaine begins with a beautiful meditation on the Carmelite as one who identifies herself completely with the Crucified One.

"A Carmelite is a soul who has gazed on the Crucified"

My dear little Germaine,

A Carmelite is a soul who has gazed on the Crucified. She has seen Him offering Himself to the Father as a Victim; and, reflecting upon this great vision of the charity of Christ, she has understood His passionate love and wanted to give herself to Him. On the mountain of Carmel, in silence, in solitude, in a prayer that never ceases, she lives as if in heaven, by God alone! The same God, who will, one day, be her beatitude and fully satisfy her glory, gives Himself to her already. He never leaves her; He dwells in her soul; even more than that, the two are but one so that she thirsts for silence so that she may always listen to Him, and penetrate more and more deeply His Infinite Being. She is identified with Him whom she loves and finds Him everywhere. Is this not heaven on earth? You carry this heaven within you, for Jesus knows the Carmelite by what is *within* her, by her soul. Never leave Him; do everything under His divine gaze and dwell joyfully in His peace and His love.

(L 133, August 1902)

Elizabeth helps Germaine to cope with the disappointment of not being able to receive Holy Communion regularly by directing her to the reality of God's living presence within, which is the essence of Carmel and can be lived in spirit before Germaine enters (see L 62 above). We recall that this is precisely what Elizabeth had to do during the long period when her mother resisted her vocation.

"Let us live in intimacy with our Beloved"

My dear little Germaine,

Let us live in intimacy with our Beloved; let us be all His as He is all ours. You are deprived of receiving Him [in Holy Communion] as often as you would wish. I understand your sacrifice, but remember that His love does not need the Sacrament in order to come to you; communicate with Him all day long since He is living in your soul. Listen to what our holy father, St. John of the Cross, tells us:

Oh, soul, most beautiful of creatures, who so ardently desires to know the place where you will find your Beloved, in order to seek Him and be united with Him. You are yourself the refuge where He takes shelter, the dwelling place where He hides Himself. Your Beloved, your Treasure, your unique Hope is so close to you that he lives within you; and it is true to say that you cannot be without him.[7]

There you have the whole life of Carmel, to live in Him. Then, all the sacrifices, the immolations become divine. Love silence and prayer, for this is the essence of our life. Ask the Queen of Carmel, our Mother, to teach you to adore Jesus in profound recollection. Pray also to our angelic Mother St. Teresa, who loved so much! . . . that she died of love! Ask her for her passion for God, for souls, because the Carmelite must be apostolic; all her prayers, all her sacrifices are for this end.

Do you know St. John of the Cross who penetrated so deeply the depths of the divinity? Before him, I should have spoken to you of St. Elijah, our first father; you see that our Order is very ancient since it goes right back to the prophets. Ah! I wish I could sing all its glories! Let us love our Order, it is incomparable! What a *Rule*! One day you will see how beautiful it is: Live it already in spirit.

(L 136, 14 September 1902)

Germaine initially wanted to be called Sister Germaine of Jesus, but has been influenced by Elizabeth's enthusiasm for the Trinity, and now wishes to be, like her mentor, Sister Germaine of the Trinity. Elizabeth's desire to live in continual communion with God gives rise to a lyrical reflection on love, which anticipates the beautiful letter to Canon Angles, L 177.

"Ask Him to make me live for love alone: this is my vocation"

My dear little sister Germaine of the Trinity,

I am "Elizabeth of the Trinity," that is to say, Elizabeth disappearing, letting herself be invaded by the "Three." Let us surrender ourselves to Them, sacrificing ourselves up to Them at every moment without seeking for anything extraordinary.

---

7. *The Spiritual Canticle* 26–27, passim, in Kavanaugh and Rodriguez, trans., *The Collected Works of St. John of the Cross*, 2nd edition (Washington: ICS, 1979), 510ff.

Let us make ourselves very small; allowing Him who is our All, to carry us in His arms as a mother does her child.

Yes, we are very weak, I would even say we are nothing but misery, but He knows that very well, He delights in forgiving us, and raising us up, in bearing us in Himself, in His purity and infinite holiness. In this way He purifies us by continual contact with Him. He wishes us to be so pure! And He himself will be our purity! We must allow ourselves to be transformed into His image, which will be accomplished simply by loving Him all the time, with a love which unites those who love. I wish to be a saint in order to glorify my Divine Master; ask Him to make me live for love alone: this is my vocation. Let us so unite ourselves to Him, that our days may be a continual communion with Him: let us wake in love, let us surrender ourselves to love all day long by doing the will of the good God, in His sight, with Him, in Him, for Him alone; let us give ourselves ceaselessly in whatever way He wishes; then, when evening comes, after an endless dialogue of love in our heart, let us sleep in love. Perhaps we will see our faults and infidelities; let us abandon them to love which is a consuming fire and thus accomplish our purgatory of love.

(L 172, August 1903)

This letter illustrates the combined influence of St. Teresa of Avila and Sister Thérèse of Lisieux: the former in her teaching on charity and the latter in her doctrine of spiritual childhood.

"Let us awaken our faith, let us remember who it is within us"

My dear little sister Germaine of the Trinity,

Since we aspire to become "victims of charity," like our holy Mother St. Teresa, we must allow ourselves to become rooted in the charity of Christ, as St. Paul says in today's beautiful epistle (Eph 3:17). And how? By always living, through everything, with Him who dwells in us, and who is Charity.

He thirsts to associate us with all that He is, to transform us into Himself. Let us awaken our faith, let us remember who it is within us and that He wants us to be very faithful to Him. How many acts of self-denial can be offered to Him, and known to Him alone. It seems to me that the saints are those souls who forget themselves all the time, who lose themselves so completely in Him whom they love, without a thought for themselves or creatures, so that they are able to say with St. Paul: "I live, yet not I, but Jesus Christ lives in me." Without doubt, we must immolate ourselves in order to arrive at this transformation, but we love sacrifice because we love the Crucified. Oh, let us look at Him attentively, let us give our soul to Him, telling Him that we long to love Him alone; that He may accomplish everything in us, because we are only little ones, and it is so good to be the good God's little child!

(L 179, 20 September 1903)

Elizabeth nearly died on Palm Sunday, and this letter, like L 266 and L 269, conveys her intense longing for death, as the moment when she will contemplate the Trinity face to face.

"To contemplate this Trinity unveiled"

My dear little sister, Germaine,

I have been in the infirmary since the end of March, with nothing to do but love God. On the evening of Palm Sunday, I had a dangerous crisis and I thought that the hour had finally arrived when I was going to fly away to the infinite realms to contemplate this Trinity unveiled. In the calm and silence of this night, I received Extreme Unction and the visit of my Master. It seemed to me that He was awaiting this moment to break my bonds. What ineffable days I spent expecting *the great Vision*! Our Reverend Mother stayed by my bedside, preparing me for the encounter with my Bridegroom and in my desire to go to Him I felt He was slow in coming. How sweet and gentle death is for those who have loved only Him and who, in the words of the Apostle, "Look not at those things which are visible because they pass, look rather to the invisible, that which is eternal!" (see 2 Cor 4:18).

(L 278, 10 June 1906)

Elizabeth's farewell letter to Germaine is particularly meaningful because of its context and content. She recalls her prayer-reflection on the Carmelite as one who has identified herself with the Crucified (L 133). This has now become a reality for Elizabeth. She exhorts Germaine not to be overwhelmed by her weakness, but to combat it with greater confidence in God.

"In the light of eternity, the good God makes me
understand many things"

Oh! If you only knew what heavenly days I spend! I am growing weaker, and I feel that it will not be long before the Divine Master comes to fetch me. I am tasting and experiencing unknown joys. How sweet and soothing are the joys of suffering. Before I die, I dream of being transformed into Jesus Crucified and this thought gives me great strength in my suffering. Our sole ideal should be to conform ourselves to this Divine Model. If the eyes of our hearts were always fixed on Him, what fervor we would then bring to our sacrifices and self-contempt. Jesus Christ dwelt in suffering during the thirty-three years He passed on earth, and His privileged ones also share in His lot. What inexpressible joy it is to think that the Father "has predestined me to be conformed to His Crucified Son" (see Rom 8:29). St. Paul has made known to us this divine election, which seems to be my portion.

In the light of eternity, the good God makes me understand many things, and I come to tell you as if it were coming from Him not to be afraid of sacrifice, of struggle, but rather to rejoice in it. If your nature is a subject of combat, a battlefield, oh, do not be discouraged, do not become sad. I would even go so far as to say love your misery, because that is where God exercises His mercy, and when the sight of it throws you into sadness and makes you withdraw into yourself, that is self-love. In times of discouragement, take refuge in the prayer of the Divine Master. He saw you and He prayed for you on the cross; this prayer of His lives and is eternally present before the Father; that prayer will save you from your miseries. The more you feel your weakness, the greater must be your confidence, because then you depend on Him alone.

(L 324, 10 October 1906)

Letters to Madame Marie Angles

While visiting Canon Angles, Elizabeth befriended his sister-in-law, Madame Marie Angles. Traumatized by an operation and ongoing ill health, and somewhat ignored by her husband, Madame Angles became nervous and withdrew into herself. Canon Angles helped her to trust in God throughout her trials and Elizabeth wrote sympathetic letters while also challenging her to welcome suffering as a valuable means of growing in union with God for the good of others. These letters, written to a woman who was nearly twice Elizabeth's age, demonstrate the maturity, conviction, and the spiritual authority of one who has suffered much herself. Elizabeth addresses the tendency to self-concern which besets many who suffer ill health, recommending a relentless war on self-preoccupation by turning one's whole attention on God. These letters thus provide a unique insight into Elizabeth's approach to suffering and a rich source of inspiration and guidance to all who desire to suffer redemptively.

Elizabeth sympathizes with the woman's distress (her niece, Marie-Louise Ambry, a close friend of Elizabeth, has lost her first baby). However, she quickly presents all Madame Angles' sufferings as tokens of God's love for her, recommending that she accept the will of God and live always with him, in accordance with her desire to follow him more closely.

"I see the will of God manifested in your sufferings"

There is no wood like the wood of the cross for enkindling the fire of love in the soul, and Jesus wants to be loved and to find in the world that so offends Him souls given to Him, that is, wholly surrendered to Him and His good pleasure. "My food is to do the will of Him who sent me" (Jn 4:34). Our Lord was the first to say this. The soul in communion with Him enters into the feelings of His divine soul, and its one ideal is to fulfill the will of the Father who has loved us from all eternity.

As you have given me leave to speak freely to you and to read something of the secrets of your heart, allow me, dear Madame, to tell you that I see the will of God manifested in your sufferings. He has deprived you of the power of action, of the ability to distract yourself or do any work, so that your one occupation may be to love and to think of Him. I tell you, from Him, that He thirsts for your soul. You are specially consecrated to Him, for, to my great joy, you wished to be His entirely while living in the world. It is so simple! He is always with you. Be always with Him, in your actions, your sufferings, and when your body is exhausted. Remain in His sight; see Him present with you, living in you.

Were I not in Carmel, I should envy your solitude; you are so secluded among your beautiful mountains. . . . How delightful to wander alone through those vast woods, to leave your books and your work, and dwell with the good God, heart-to-heart, in close intimacy, gazing upon Him with overflowing love! Enjoy such happiness; it is heavenly.

(L 138, September 1902)

In Dijon Carmel at that time, only the recreation room was heated, so the cold was intense. Elizabeth, who felt the cold terribly, copes because she loves her Divine Master. One of her favorite, oft-cited Scripture quotations appears here for the first time in her letters, Ephesians 2:4. Elizabeth repeats her ideal of a Carmelite which she described to Germaine de Gemeaux in L 133: "A soul who has gazed on the Crucified."

"Because of 'His exceeding love' for us" (see Eph 2:4)

You ask me how I can endure the cold. Believe me, I am not more generous than you are, but you are ill and I am in good health. I do not feel the cold, so you see I have little merit. I used to suffer far more from winter when I was at home than I do in Carmel without a fire. The good God gives us the grace. Besides, it is good for us to feel such little things, to look at the Divine Master who also endured all these things because of "His exceeding love" for us; then we long to return Him love for love. We meet with many such sacrifices in Carmel, but they are sweet when the heart is wholly taken up with love.

I will tell you what I do when I feel a little tired: I look at the Divine Crucified, and when I see how He gave Himself for me, it seems that I can do no less than spend myself, wear myself out in order to repay Him a little of what He has given me. Dear Madame, during Holy Mass each morning, let us be in communion with His sacrifice. We are His brides; we ought to be like Him. Then, throughout the day, let us remain always with Him. If we faithfully live His life, if we identify with all the movements of the soul of the divine Crucified, we need no longer fear our weaknesses; He will be our strength, and who will dare to take us from Him? I believe that He is greatly pleased with you, and that your sacrifices must console His Heart. During Lent, let our rendezvous be the infinity of God, in His charity. Would you like that to be the desert where, with our Divine Bridegroom, we will live in profound solitude, since it is in this solitude that He speaks to our hearts?

(L 156, 15 February 1903)

Elizabeth wrote this letter to thank Madame Angles for her greetings on the feast of St. Elizabeth. She reflects on the wisdom of the saints, who see things in the light of eternity, and inspire us to follow their example. She anticipates Pope John Paul II's appreciation of the role of the saints in the church as models, guides, and intercessors.

"Let us ask Him to be Himself our sanctity"

It is good for us to look into the soul of the saints and to
follow them, in faith, right up to heaven. There they shine
with the light of God, whom they contemplate face to face.
This heaven of the saints is our homeland, the Father's house,
where we are awaited and loved, and where, one day, we too
will fly and rest in the bosom of infinite Love. When we fix
our eyes on the divine world which already surrounds us, even
in our earthly exile, then the things of this world simply disappear! They are the things that are not, they are less than
nothing. The saints fully understood this true wisdom, which
makes us leave all things, ourselves above all, to fly to God and
dwell in Him alone. Dear Madame, He dwells in us to sanctify
us. Let us ask Him to be Himself our sanctity. The Gospel tells
us that when Our Lord was on earth, a "secret power" went
out from Him: at His touch, the sick were healed and the dead
were raised to life. Well! He is still living, living in the taberna-
cle, in the adorable Sacrament, living in our souls. He Himself
said: "Those who love me will keep my word, and my Father
will love them, and we will come to them, and make our home
with them" (Jn 14:23). Since He is there, let us keep Him company as the lover does with one he loves. This divine union is
wholly interior: it is the essence of the Carmelite life which
makes our solitude so dear to us, for, as our father, St. John
of the Cross, whose feast we are celebrating today, says; "Two
hearts that love one another prefer solitude above all else."[8]

On Saturday, the Feast of the Presentation of Our Lady, we
had the beautiful ceremony of the renewal of our vows. Oh!
dear Madame, what a beautiful day that was! What a joy to
bind oneself to the service of so kind a Master, to tell Him that
one is His till death, the bride of Christ! I am very happy to

8. Ibid. 36:1, 545.

know that you, too, are given to Him. I think that our great St. Elizabeth in heaven must bless and seal the union of our souls.

I shall never again see your beautiful mountains, but in heart and soul I shall follow you there, asking Him who is our rendezvous to draw us to those other mountains, to those divine summits so far distant from the earth that they nearly touch heaven. It is there that I remain united with you beneath the rays of the Sun of Love!

(L 184, November 1903)

Elizabeth had a great love of prayer and adoration before the Blessed Sacrament, a strong tradition in French Carmels, and which she considered an expression of love. Her invitation to "live a Lent of love together," provides a refreshingly positive perspective on this rich season.

"Let us begin our heaven on earth, our heaven in love!"

I have felt particularly close to you during these past few days as I have been reading the life of St. Elizabeth, your mother and my heavenly patroness. I am so fond of these words addressed to her by Our Lord: "Elizabeth, if you want to be with Me, I want to be with you, and nothing can separate us." Dear Madame, did not the Divine Bridegroom speak these words to us in the silence of our soul, when He invited us to follow Him more closely, to be one with Him by becoming His brides? During these days when we keep the "Forty Hours" we have the Blessed Sacrament exposed in the oratory. Today, Sunday, I have spent nearly the whole day before Our Lord, trying by my love to make Him forget the sins committed during these days of carnival.

Lent begins on Wednesday; would you like to make a Lent of love together? "He loved me and gave Himself for me" (Gal 2:20). This then is the aim of love: to give oneself, to empty ourselves entirely into Him whom we love. "Love makes the lover go out of himself, transporting him, by an ineffable ecstasy, into the Heart of Him who loves." Isn't this a beautiful thought? Let it be the guiding light of our souls, so that they may let themselves be carried away by the Spirit of love, and in the light of faith, may they even now join in the hymn of love eternally sung by the blessed before the throne of the Lamb. Yes, dear Madame, let us begin our heaven on earth, our Heaven in love! He Himself is this love, as St. John tells us: "God is love" (1 Jn 4:8). Shall not this be our place of rendezvous?

(L 194, February 1904)

Elizabeth shares her own New Year's resolutions, to become holy through union with the will of God. We see the influence of her "Prayer to the Trinity" in this letter and her by now favorite name, "Praise of Glory."

"If you bear this state of powerlessness with fidelity
and love, you can cover Him with glory"

While I was reading the epistles of St. Peter I came across a quotation which will express the good wishes of your little Carmelite friend: "In your hearts sanctify Christ as Lord" (1 Pt 3:15). To do that we must carry out the words of St. John the Baptist: "He must increase, but I must decrease" (Jn 3:30). Dear Madame, let us make God increase in our souls during this new year which He gives us to sanctify ourselves and to unite ourselves more closely with Him. Let us keep Him "alone and set apart"; let Him truly be King. As for us, let self disappear and be forgotten, that we may be nothing but the "Praise of His glory," according to the Apostle's beautiful expression.

I also wish you all the blessings of health which you need, as you suffer so much in this respect. Remember what St. Paul said, "So, I will boast all the more gladly of my weaknesses, so that the power of Christ may dwell in me" (2 Cor 12:9). It is all in the will of God. In your physical sufferings that affect your soul as well, rejoice, dear Madame, and remember that if you bear this state of powerlessness with fidelity and love, you can

cover Him with glory. Our holy Mother St. Teresa said: "When
we know how to unite ourselves to God and to His holy will,
accepting whatever He wishes, we are happy for we possess
everything."[9]

I wish you this deep peace in the divine good pleasure.
I understand what sacrifices your health must impose upon
you, but it is sweet to say to oneself: "This is what He wills."
He said one day, to one of His saints, "Drink, eat, sleep, do
whatever you like, *as long as you love Me.*" It is love that makes
His yoke so easy and His burden so light. Let us ask the Divine
Infant to consume us by His divine flame, by the fire that He
willed to bring on earth. . . .

(L 220, January 1905)

*Elizabeth reassures Madame Angles of the community's prayer,
which supports her as she faces another operation. Whatever the cir-
cumstances, Elizabeth urges her friend to trust God.*

"Launch your soul upon the waves
of confidence and abandonment"

Before entering the great silence of Lent, our Reverend
Mother has allowed me to tell you how earnestly my dear community and I are praying for you. I understand your dread of
an operation, and beg Our Lord to relieve and calm your fears
Himself. The apostle St. Paul says that God "accomplishes all
things according to his counsel and will" (Eph 1:11); consequently we must receive everything as coming directly from
the divine hand of our Father, who loves us and who, in the
midst of all our trials, pursues His goal of uniting us more intimately with Himself. Launch your soul upon the waves of confidence and abandonment; remember that whatever troubles
or frightens you does not come from the good God because

---

9. Not an actual quotation from St. Teresa.

He is the "Prince of Peace," that peace which He has prom-ised to all those of good will. You tell me that you fear you have abused His graces; well that is the time to redouble your confidence, for "where sin increased, grace abounded all the more" (Rom 5:20), and "God . . . is rich in mercy, out of the great love with which He loved us" (Eph 2:4). Have no fear then of that hour through which we must all pass. Death, dear Madame, is the sleep of a child resting upon its mother's heart. At last the night of exile will have fled forever and we shall enter into possession of "the inheritance of the saints in light" (Col 1:12). St. John of the Cross says that we shall be judged on love, which corresponds to what Our Lord said of St. Mary Magdalene: "Her sins, which were many, have been forgiven; hence she has shown great love" (Lk 7:47). I often think that I shall have a very long purgatory, for much will be asked of the one who has received much, and He has been so generous to His little bride! But then I abandon myself to His love and while still here below, I sing the hymn of His mercies.

If we were to grow more like God every day, with what assurance should we regard the hour in which we must appear before His infinite holiness. I believe that you have discovered the secret. It is by self-denial that we reach this divine end; by this we die to self and make space for God. Do you remem-ber the beautiful passage in St. John's Gospel where Our Lord says to Nicodemus, "Very truly, I tell you, no one can see the kingdom of God without being born from above" (Jn 3:3)? Let us renew ourselves in the depths of our soul, "seeing that you have stripped off the old self with its practices and have clothed yourselves with the new self, which is being renewed in knowledge according to the image of its creator" (Col 3:9–10). It is to be done gently and simply, by separating ourselves from all that is not God. Then the soul no longer fears nor desires anything for its will is entirely lost in the will of God, and this is what creates union.

Let us pray much for one another during the holy season of Lent, retiring into the desert with our Master, and asking Him to teach us to live His life.

(L 224, March 1905)

This advice on how Madame Angles was to endure great physical and interior suffering gives us an insight into how Elizabeth dealt with her own interior difficulties in the novitiate and how she would deal with the physical sufferings of her protracted illness.

"Try then, in your will, to be wholly joyful under
the hand that crucifies you"

I think that the secret of peace and happiness lies in forgetfulness and disregard of self, which does not mean that we do not feel our physical or mental sufferings. Since you allow me to speak to you like a sister, it seems to me that God is asking you for abandonment and unlimited trust. At those times when you feel those terrible voids, believe that He is hollowing out in your soul greater capacities to receive Him, capacities which are, to an extent, as infinite as Himself. Try then, in your will, to be wholly joyful under the hand that crucifies you; I would even go so far as to say that you should look upon each suffering as a proof of love that comes to you directly from God in order to unite you to Him. Do not be discouraged when your soul is oppressed and wearied by the burden of your body, but have recourse by faith and love to Him who said: "Come to me . . . and I will give you rest" (Mt 11:28). Never let yourself be depressed by the thought of your wretchedness. The great St. Paul said: "Where sin increased, grace abounded all the more" (Rom 5:20). So it seems to me that the weakest, even the most sinful person has the greatest right to hope. By forgetting self and casting herself into the arms of God, she glorifies Him more than any self-examination or self-reproach, which keeps her attention fixed on her defects even though she possesses at her very center a Savior who is willing to purify her.

Do you remember that beautiful passage where Jesus said to His Father: "you have given Him authority over all people that He may give eternal life to all whom you have given Him" (Jn 17:2)? That is what He wants to do in us. He wants you to go out of yourself, to give up all that preoccupies you, in order to withdraw into the solitude He has chosen as His dwelling place in the depths of your heart. He is always there, even when you do not feel it. He is waiting for you and wants to establish a "wonderful exchange" with you, as we sing in the beautiful liturgy, the intimacy between bride and Bridegroom. Through this continual contact with you, He can deliver you from your weaknesses, your faults, from all that troubles you. Nothing can prevent you going to Him.

It does not matter whether you are feeling fervent or discouraged: we pass from one state to another in this earthly exile. You must believe that He never changes; that in His care for you He is always bending over you, longing to bear you away and establish you within Himself. If, in spite of all your efforts you are overcome with sadness, unite your agony to that of the Divine Master in the Garden of Olives, when He said to His Father: "If it is possible, let this cup pass from me" (Mt 26:39). Perhaps you think it is difficult to forget yourself. Do not be anxious about that, it is extremely simple. I will tell you my secret: think about God who dwells in you, whose temple you are. St. Paul tells us this and we can believe him. Little by little, the soul becomes accustomed to living in His blessed company; realizing that it bears within it a little heaven where the God of love has made His home. From then on, the spirit breathes a divine atmosphere; indeed, only the body seems to be on earth, while the soul lives beyond the veil, with Him who is Unchanging.

Do not say that such a thing is not for you, that you are too miserable a creature, for that is all the more reason why you should go to your Savior. We shall never be purified by looking at our own misery, but by gazing on Him who is purity and holiness itself.

When you feel very unhappy, think to yourself that the Divine Sculptor is using the chisel to beautify His work and remain peacefully under the hand that shapes you. After St. Paul had been carried off to the third heaven, he felt his own infirmity and complained about it to God, who answered: "My grace is sufficient for you; for power is made perfect in weakness" (2 Cor 12:9). Isn't that very consoling? Be of good heart! I entrust you in a special way to the care of a little Carmelite nun of Lisieux, Sister Thérèse of the Child Jesus who died at the age of twenty-four, in the odor of sanctity. She had a special grace to enlarge souls, launching them on the waves of love, confidence and abandonment. She says that she found happiness when she began to *forget herself*. Will you join me in praying to her every day for the wisdom that makes saints and brings the soul great peace and happiness?

(L 249, 24 November 1905)

Elizabeth encourages Madame Angles to offer herself unreservedly to God because abandonment to God's will is the "secret" of holiness.

"You see now how much you can glorify Him in these states of suffering and listlessness that are so difficult to bear!" May 1906 be for your soul a chain of fidelity in which each link, soldered by love, may unite you more intimately to the Divine Master, and make you truly His captive, "in chains," as St. Paul says. In his great and generous heart, he wished for his followers, "that Christ may dwell in your hearts through faith, as you are being rooted and grounded in love" (Eph 3:17). That is what I wish for you, too, dear Madame: that the reign of love may be fully established in your interior kingdom, and that the weight of this love may make you totally oblivious of self, and conduct you to that mystic death of which the Apostle spoke when he exclaimed: "It is no longer I who live, but it is Christ who lives in me" (Gal 2:20). The Divine Master, in his discourse after the Last Supper, that last love song of the Master's soul, utters to the Father those beautiful words: "I glorified you on earth by finishing the work that you gave me to do" (Jn 17:4). We are His brides, dear Madame, and consequently, ought to identify ourselves totally with Him, and ought to be able to repeat these same words at the close of each day. Perhaps you will ask me, how are we to glorify Him? It is very simple. Our Lord told us the secret when He said: "My food is to do the will of Him who sent me" (Jn 4:34). Be devoted then to the will of this adorable Master; look at every suffering and every joy as coming directly from Him, and then your life will be a continual Communion, since everything will be like a sacrament that will give you God. This is very real, because God is not divided; His will is His whole being. He is wholly and entirely in all things and these things are, to a certain extent, nothing but an emanation of His love! You see now how much you can glorify Him in these states of suffering and listlessness that are so difficult to bear! Forget yourself as much as you can, for that is the secret of peace and happiness. St. Francis Xavier exclaimed: "What concerns me, concerns me not; what concerns Him, concerns me deeply."[10] How happy is the soul which has reached such complete detachment; that is love indeed!

July 2018
(L 264, January 1906)

Letters to Abbé André Chevignard

Abbé André Chevignard, a seminarian almost the same age as Elizabeth, was the younger brother of Guite's husband, Georges, who introduced them. After he visited Elizabeth in Dijon Carmel, she wrote to Guite that there had been a "fusion" between the souls of the priest and

---

10. Source unknown.

the Carmelite, a bond of grace, closer than any ties of blood relationship. He became a "soul friend," with whom Elizabeth reflected on their different, yet similar, vocations: two young people, priest and Carmelite, wholly given to God. It is to Abbé Chevignard that Elizabeth first confides her "new name," "Praise of Glory," which she discovered in the writings of St. Paul in January 1904.

Elizabeth's love of deep, listening silence radiates from this extract. For her, silence was not an absence of words but presence, relationship, love.

"The mission of the Carmelite and the priest . . . show forth God and give Him to souls"

Do you not have a passion to listen to Him? Sometimes it is so strong, this need to be silent, that I would like to do nothing else but remain at the Savior's feet, like Magdalene, eager to hear everything and to penetrate more and more deeply the mystery of charity that He came to reveal. Have you not found that while we are active and appear to be filling Martha's role, the soul can remain buried in contemplation, like Magdalene, like a thirsty man near the fountain? That seems to me to be the mission of the Carmelite and the priest: both can show forth God and give Him to souls if they are always close to the Divine source. I think we should draw very near to the Master, and be in communion with His soul, identifying ourselves with all its impulses, then go forth, like Him, according to the will of His Father.

(L 158, 24 February 1903)

Carmelites neither write nor receive letters during Advent, Lent, or retreats, in order to recollect themselves more fully and become more deeply immersed in the mysteries of Christ's life, celebrated liturgically by the church. Elizabeth writes this letter before the beginning of Advent, sharing her growing understanding of her name-vocation.

"To lose myself, be transformed then . . . I should really be 'Elizabeth *of the Trinity*'"

When I think of my name, my soul is carried away by the great vision of the mystery of mysteries into that Trinity which even in this world is our cloister, our dwelling place, the infinite Being enclosed in which we can pass through everything. I am just reading the beautiful teaching of our father St. John of the Cross about the transformation of the soul into the Three Divine Persons. To what sublime glory we are called! I can understand the silence and recollection of the saints who could not withdraw from their contemplation, so that God could lead them to the divine summits where union is made perfect between Him and the soul, which is His mystic bride.

What an adorable mystery of charity that God should call us, by our vocation, to live in this holy light! . . . I should like to respond to it by passing through this world like Our Lady, "keeping all these things in my heart," burying myself, as it were, in the depths of my soul, so as to lose myself, to be transformed into the Blessed Trinity Who dwells there; then my motto, "my luminous ideal," as you call it, would be realized and I should really be "Elizabeth *of the Trinity*."

(L 185, 28 November 1903)

Elizabeth reflects on the implications of our baptism: as Christians, we share in the prayer of Christ.

"Two words sum up for me all holiness, all apostolate:
'Union and Love'"

Since Our Lord dwells in our souls, His prayer is ours, and I desire to live there in unceasing communion with Him, like a little vase at the Source, so that I may be able to give life to others by letting His infinite streams of charity overflow on them. "And for their sakes I sanctify myself, so that they also may be sanctified in truth" (Jn 17:19). Let us make these words of our adored Master all our own; yes, let us sanctify ourselves for souls, and since we are all members of one body, then in the measure that we have the divine life within us, we can communicate it to the great body of the Church.

There are two words that sum up for me all holiness, all apostolate: "Union and Love." Ask that I may live that fully, and for that purpose, dwell completely hidden away in the Holy Trinity; you could not wish anything more beautiful for me! . . .

(L 191, 25 January 1904)

On hearing of the death of his father, Elizabeth consoles her friend with the example of Christ's tears and comforts him with the knowledge of his father's goodness.

"Our only comfort can come from the Master"

I have heard of the painful sacrifice God asks of you. I think that, at such times, our only comfort can come from the Master whose divinely loving Heart "was troubled" at the tomb of Lazarus, so that we can weep with Him and, leaning on Him, find fresh strength and peace. I pray a great deal for your father's soul. He was indeed the "just man" of whom the Scriptures speak. What a consolation, when his course was run, to look back on a life so full of good works! For him the veil has fallen, the darkness of mystery has disappeared: he has seen! . . . Let us follow him, in faith, into the regions of peace and love, for all must end in God, who some day will say His "*Veni*" to us also. Then, like the babe on its mother's breast, we shall sleep in Him, and "in His light we shall see light" (see Ps 36:9).

A Dieu, Monsieur l'Abbé. Let us live on the heights far away . . . in Him . . . in our hearts, and as the communion of saints brings us into contact with those who have left us, let us pray together for the soul of your dear father, so that if he has not yet attained it, he may soon enjoy the eternal vision of God. I remain united to you under the radiance of the Face of God.

(L 200, April 1904)

Elizabeth was delighted to have been baptized on the feast of St.
Mary Magdalene, July 22.

"The feast of my soul"

Tomorrow is the feast of St. Mary Magdalene, she of whom
Truth said: "She has loved much," and it is also the feast of my
soul, for I celebrate the anniversary of my baptism; and since
you are the priest of love, I beg you to consecrate me to Him
at Holy Mass. Baptize me in the Blood of the Lamb, so that,
purified of all that is not Him, I may love Him alone with an
ever-growing passion, until I reach that blessed union which
God has predestined for us in His eternal and unchanging will.

(L 234, 21 July 1905)

This is the first time that Elizabeth associates "sacrifice" with her
new name, "Praise of Glory." Emerging in the context of the Eucharist,
it indicates her growing sacramental spirituality.

"God has united our souls so that we should help one another"

This evening I am starting on a long journey, which is nothing less than my private retreat. I shall be in absolute solitude
for the next ten days, with several extra hours for prayer, and
I shall wear our veil down when walking around the monastery. I shall be more than ever like a hermit in the desert. Before
entering my Thebaid, I feel a real need to ask for the help of
your good prayers, above all a special intention in the Holy
Sacrifice of the Mass. When you consecrate the host in which
Jesus, who alone is the Holy One, is about to become incarnate,
would you consecrate me with Him, "as a sacrifice of praise to
His glory," so that all my aspirations, all my movements, all my
actions may be a homage rendered to His holiness?

"You shall be holy, for I the Lord your God am holy . . ."
(Lev 19:2). I recollect myself with these words, and beneath
their light I shall make my divine journey. St. Paul comments on
these words for me, when he says: "He chose us in Him before

the foundation of the world to be holy and blameless before Him in love" (Eph 1:4). This, then, is the secret of virginal purity: to dwell in love, that is to say, in God: "God is love" (1 Jn 4:16). I count on you to pray much for me during these ten days. Indeed, it seems to me quite simple, for has He not said: "A brother who is helped by his brother is like a strong city" (see Prov 18:19)?[11] I entrust this mission to you. Monsieur l'Abbé, would you offer for me St. Paul's fervent prayer for his beloved Ephesians? "That, according to the riches of His glory, He may grant that you may be strengthened in your inner being with power through His Spirit . . ." (Eph 3:16–19).

"Let us sanctify Christ in our hearts" (see 1 Pt 3:15) so as to realize what David sang under the influence of the Holy Spirit: "Upon him my holiness will shine" (see Ps 132:18).

(L 244, 8 October 1905)

Elizabeth reflects on Advent as a holy season particularly precious to contemplatives and all "interior souls" who strive to live constantly in the presence of God. Her identification of the life of priest and Carmelite is a profound insight into the apostolic fruitfulness of both vocations in the Mystical Body of Christ, the church. When Abbé Chevignard took up his first post as curate, Elizabeth wrote a letter reminding him that, through her prayer, she was the "curate of the curate."

"The life of the priest and the Carmelite is an advent"

I like the thought that the life of the priest and the Carmelite is an advent that prepares souls for the Incarnation. David says in one of the psalms: "Fire goes before him" (Ps 97:3). Is not love that fire? And is it not also our mission to prepare the way of the Savior by our union with Him whom the

---

11. Elizabeth, probably copying from Sister Thérèse, misquotes this verse which should read, "An ally offended is stronger than a city." See Clarke, trans., *Story of a Soul: The Autobiography of Saint Thérèse of Lisieux*, 3rd ed. (Washington: ICS Publications, 1996), 236.

Apostle calls a consuming fire? By contact with Him, our soul will become a flame of love, spreading throughout all the members of the Body of Christ, which is the Church. Then we shall console our Master's Heart, and He will be able to show us to His Father, saying: "I am already glorified in them" (Jn 17:10).

(L 250, 29 November 1905)

Letters to Mother Germaine of Jesus

Mother Germaine of Jesus was novice mistress when Elizabeth first entered. Soon after, although only thirty-one years old, she was elected to lead the community and she remained prioress and spiritual guide throughout Elizabeth's time in Carmel. Mother Germaine quickly recognized Elizabeth's holiness and accompanied her with great love and spiritual sensitivity throughout the final months of her life.

Elizabeth described her bed as an "altar," herself as "victim," and Mother Germaine as her "priest," assisting in the offering of the Mass of her life.

"I feel the power of your priesthood"
from "The Palace of Suffering and Beatitude"

My darling Mother, my beloved priest,
Oh, help me to climb my Calvary; I feel the power of your priesthood over my soul so strongly, and I need you so much. Mother, I feel my Three so close to me; I am more overwhelmed by happiness than by pain: my Master has reminded me that it is my dwelling place and I am not to choose my sufferings; so I immerse myself with Him into immense suffering, with much fear and anguish.

(L 320, October 1906)

She actually told Mother Germaine that her suffering was so great that she could understand how people committed suicide. Yet she also experienced peace.

"She feels so cowardly"

My beloved priest,

Your victim is suffering very, very much; it is a kind of physical agony. She feels so cowardly, cowardly enough to scream! But the Being who is the Fullness of Love visits her, keeping her company.

(L 329, October 1906)

Elected prioress of Dijon Carmel eight times, Mother Germaine was a fine religious and an excellent leader, yet she experienced a certain diffidence about her own ability, often the case with sensitive characters. This letter was found by Mother Germaine after Elizabeth's death, and only discovered among Mother Germaine's papers after her death in 1934. It is Elizabeth's "final word" to her and us.

"Let yourself be loved"

When you read these lines, your little "Praise of Glory" will no longer be singing on earth, but will be living in the immense furnace of Love. . . . Your child is coming to you to reveal what she feels, or more truly, what God, in those hours of profound recollection and unifying contact, has helped her to understand: "You are uncommonly loved," loved with that love of preference that the Master, here below, had for some and which carried them so far. He does not say to you, as He said to Peter: "Do you love me more than these?" Mother, listen to what He tells you: "Let yourself be loved more than these." That is to say, without fearing that any obstacle may be a hindrance because I am free to pour out my love on whom I wish. . . . That is your vocation; in being faithful to it you will make me happy because you will thus magnify the power of my love. This love can rebuild what has been destroyed.

Mother, let yourself be loved more than the others, that explains everything and prevents the soul from being surprised; if you will allow her, your little host will spend her Heaven in the depths of your soul, she will keep you in communion with Love, believing in Love; this will be the sign of her dwelling in you. Oh! in what intimacy we shall live! My Mother, may your life also be spent in the heavens, there where I will sing in your name the eternal *Sanctus*; I will do nothing without you before the throne of God; you well know that I bear your imprint and that something of yourself appeared with your infant before the Face of God. I also ask that you do nothing without me, you have granted me this. I will come to live in you, I will instruct you, so that you will profit from my vision and participate in it, so that you too may live the life of the blessed. . . . I bequeath you this vocation which was mine in the heart of the Church Militant and which I will unceasingly fulfill in the Church Triumphant: "The Praise of Glory of the Holy Trinity."

Mother, let yourself be loved, more than these others; it is in this way that your Master wishes you to be a praise of His glory. He rejoices to build up in you, through His love, and it is He alone who wants to work in you. . . . He will do all in you; He will go right to the end. . . . Live in the depths of your soul. My Master makes me understand so clearly that He wants to create marvelous things there; you are called to render homage to the simplicity of the Divine Being and to magnify the power of His Love.

(L 337, October 1906)

Letters to Other Correspondents

We see Elizabeth's deeply affectionate nature in her letters to Madame de Sourdon, mother of Françoise and a great friend of the Catez family: she writes several times that she loved Madame de Sourdon, "like a mother," and called herself her "third daughter." A widow, she anguished over Françoise's volatile temperament and the difficulty of finding a husband for her daughter Marie-Louise. Elizabeth assured her of prayers for this intention which would continue after her death.

Letters to Madame de Sourdon

This extract contains one of the most profound messages associated with Elizabeth of the Trinity.

"I would like to share this secret with all those I love"

I have found heaven on earth, since heaven is God and God is in my soul. The day I understood that, everything became clear to me, and I would like to share this secret with all those I love so that they, too, might cling to God through everything, so that this prayer of Christ might be fulfilled: "Father, may they be made perfectly one!"

(L 122, 15 June 1902)

Elizabeth's spirituality is firmly in the tradition of St. Francis de Sales. Like him, she encourages her friends, people in every walk of life, to strive for holiness. There is a particular poignancy in the mention of her own suffering. She is probably referring to her mother's objection to her entering Carmel which resulted in such a long and painful delay.

"This 'better part' which seems my privilege in my beloved solitude in Carmel, is offered by God to every Christian soul."

Your kind letter pained me, for I feel how profoundly sad you are. I have prayed much for you, and have communicated with the Word of Life, with Him who came to bring consolation for all our sorrows and who, on the eve of His passion, in that discourse after the Last Supper during which He poured out His soul said, in speaking of those who were His own: "That they may have my joy made complete in themselves" (Jn 17:13). Abandonment, dear Madame, that is what gives us to God. I am very young, yet it seems to me that I have really suffered at times. Oh! then, when everything was dark, when the present was so painful and when the future looked even more somber, I closed my eyes, and abandoned myself, like a child, in the arms of this Father who is in heaven.

Dear Madame, will you allow this little Carmelite who loves you so dearly to tell you something on behalf of the Divine Master? These are the words He spoke to St. Catherine of Siena: "Think of Me and I will think of you." We look at ourselves too much; we want to see and understand; we do not have enough confidence in Him who enfolds us in His love. We must not stand before the cross and look at it in itself, but recollecting ourselves in the light of faith, we must rise above it, and consider it as the instrument which is used by Divine Love. "One thing alone is necessary. Mary has chosen the better part, which will not be taken away from her" (Lk 10:42). This "better part," which seems my privilege in my beloved solitude in Carmel, is offered by God to every Christian soul. He offers it to you, dear Madame, among all your cares and anxieties. You must always believe that His sole desire is to lead you more and more deeply into Himself. Surrender yourself to Him with all your preoccupations.

(L 129, 25 July 1902)

Letter to Madame Hallo

The Hallo and Catez families were next-door neighbors who became lifelong friends; Elizabeth also called Madame Hallo a "second mama"; Marie-Louise was her best friend and "sister," and she regarded Charles as a "little brother." When the Hallo family moved to Paris, Madame Catez often visited them. Elizabeth commends her "second mama" for her indefatigable work for the church.

"What a consolation to give God to souls and souls to God!"

I know that you work with untiring zeal for the greater glory of God. That, in one form or another, ought to be the work of our life, it is our "predestination," according to the words of St. Paul. May this New Year be a year of love, consecrated to the glory of God. How happy we should be on the last day if we could say with our adored Master: "I glorified you on earth by finishing the work that you gave me to do" (Jn 17:4). What a consolation to give God to souls and souls to God! Life becomes something completely different when we look at it from this point of view. From the depths of my cell, I follow you everywhere and I commend you to the Father of the family, "those two" who are working so well on His house, while I am their little "Moses" on the mountain. . . .

(L 218, January 1905)

Letter to Madame Berthe Gout de Bize

Only weeks before dying, Elizabeth writes to another friend, assuring her that she will continue praying, in heaven, for a husband for her daughter, Jaja. As always, in Elizabeth's letters we have a wonderful combination of humanity and spirituality: they are one and the same in the saints.

"A Being called Love"

Perhaps God is waiting for me to go to Heaven to arrange her future with the Blessed Virgin. . . . I confide to you what has made my life an anticipated Heaven: believing that a Being called Love dwells in us at every moment of the day and night and that He asks us to live in communion with Him, to receive every joy, like every suffering, equally as coming directly from His love.

(L 330, October 1906)

Letter to Madame de Bobet

Elizabeth knows that she is dying and in this last letter to another dear friend leaves an inspiring spiritual testament.

"I leave you my faith in the presence of God"

I leave you my faith in the presence of God, of the God who is all love, dwelling in our souls. I confide to you: it is this intimacy with Him "within" that has been the beautiful sun illuminating my life, making it already an anticipated Heaven; it is what sustains me today in my suffering.

(L 333, October 1906)

Letter to Sister Marie-Odile

Sister Marie-Odile was an extern sister who befriended Elizabeth when she was a "postulant outside the walls." She moved to the new foundation at Paray-le-Monial, and they wrote to each other. Unfortunately, Sister Marie-Odile destroyed most of Elizabeth's letters. This one from Elizabeth is particularly important.

"If I started my life over again, oh,
I would wish not to waste one instant!"

I think that in heaven my mission will be to draw souls by helping them go out of themselves to cling to God by a wholly simple and loving movement, and to keep them in this great silence within that will allow God to communicate Himself to them and transform them into Himself. Dear little sister of my soul, it seems to me that I now see everything in God's light, and if I started my life over again, oh, I would wish not to waste one instant! He does not allow us, His brides in Carmel, to devote ourselves to anything but love, but the divine, and if by chance, in the radiance of His light, I see you leave that sole occupation, I will come very quickly to call you to order; you would want that, wouldn't you? . . . Beloved little sister, let us live by love so that we may die of love and glorify the God who is all Love.

(L 335, 28 October 1906)

Poems

Right: 18 years old

Left: "I was thinking of Him while it was taken, so it will bring Him to you."

Introduction

*E*lizabeth started writing "poems" at the age of fourteen, while on holiday with her Rolland aunts at Carlipa. Seventy-two remain of those she wrote before entering Carmel, and a further fifty-one written after. While she expressed herself spontaneously in verse, she would not have considered herself a "poet." St. Teresa of Avila, foundress of the Carmelites, encouraged her sisters to write "verses," which could be sung to popular tunes, in order to entertain the community at recreation on special liturgical feasts such as Christmas and celebrations such as a clothing or profession. Many of Elizabeth's Carmelite verses name the melody they fit. The resulting compositions were not intended to be literary masterpieces. Elizabeth's attempts to make her verses rhyme led to a certain forced quality and repetition of easily rhyming words which is evident in the French originals. Bouyer derides Elizabeth's (and Thérèse's) poems, as "consistently atrocious,"[1] but that is to miss the point. As Elizabeth's community noted, the value of her poems lies in what they disclose of her spirituality and fervor. They reveal much about her inner journey.

The poems written in Carmel vary both in content and quality. The earlier ones, P 73–96, show her love and understanding of her Carmelite vocation. Those written from the infirmary during the last eight months of her life, P 97–123, are of a different caliber. The English translations of the following, except for P 113, are by Alan Bancroft, from his "Barb of Fire: Twenty Poems of Blessed Elizabeth of the Trinity, with selected passages from Blessed Columba Marmion, O.S.B." His translations reflect closely the rhyme, meter, and intent of Elizabeth's French texts. They appear here by kind permission of the publishers, Gracewing, Leominster, England.

---

1. Louis Bouyer, *Women Mystics* (San Francisco: Ignatius Press, 1993), 156.

The Heaven of Glory and the Heaven of Faith

This poem, a dialogue between heaven and Earth, written for Mother Germaine's feast, was one of Elizabeth's favorites. Sister Agnes said they often sang it together while working in the garden during recreation.

Voice of Heaven

We who are bathed in Light, within the 'Three'—
The Face of God, the splendor of its rays—
See, by those shinings, into Mystery:
They ever show new secrets, Heaven's days.

Infinite Being! Depth unsoundable!
Delighted, *lost* in Your Divinity—
O Trinity, God thrice-immutable,
We see Yourself in Your own clarity.

Voice of Earth

The saints in Heav'n . . . but, also, here below
Souls come and merge themselves in such a Love,
In mystery and night this happens so—
God satisfies: in dark, in Day above.

Through everything . . . on earth: already we're
Possessing You, our Peace and vision! (for,
As in one light we gather, there and here,
We lose ourselves in God, for evermore!)

Voice of Heaven

As sharers, *now*, in God's own Essence, you
Possess all we possess in Heaven . . . See!—
You have not yet the joy we have, that's true:
But as for giving—you give more than we.

And when one loves, how good it is to give!
(You *can* be giving, every hour and place.)
Oh, give God glory while on earth you live—
By self-oblation. Seize on this high grace!

(P 80, June 1902)

The Carmelite

This poem was written in the first year of Elizabeth's novitiate, feast of the non-choir sisters, July 29, 1902. It gives us an insight into Elizabeth's understanding of the Carmelite life and has echoes of a favorite idea: the Carmelite is a "sacrament of Christ."

She's one self-given, is a Carmelite—
A sacrifice, who's wholly occupied
To render God His glory (yet how bright
Her calvary! with Jesus, crucified).
Having her God, a Victim, in her gaze,
Light flashed within her soul, and that is why,
Knowing her soaring mission in its rays,
She cried, her wounded heart cried, "Here am I!"

A Carmelite is one invaded: how?
Christ-filled, she's one who can, unceasingly,
Give Christ; for God made choice of her, and now
Like Mary, always at His feet she'll be.
Look well, then, at this captive who remains
In prayer that knows no interruption: for,
Soul caught and taken, she is now in chains—
Her Christ, and no distraction any more!

A Carmelite, a soul adoring! one
Surrendered to God's action, all, entire;
Whatever comes—in Large Communion,
Her heart uplifted, burning with God's fire!
'The one thing necessary' she has found:
God's Being, Light and Love. She'll intercede—
Her prayer a cloak that wraps the world around:
In that way—an apostle then indeed!

This, too: a soul that's closed, a Carmelite—
Closed up to things that happen here below;
Yet, also, wholly open and alight
To look on what the eye can never know.

And God, the Eagle, bears her in the air—
His light upon high summits like the sun—
To give her roof, the Father's dwelling there,
With God; consumed entirely, with Him one!

(P 83, July 1902)

Carmelites have the tradition of writing Christmas "verses" to be sung during community recreation. Elizabeth wrote this poem for Christmas 1903. "Amo Christum" [I love Christ], the motto of Dijon Carmel, was inscribed on the crossbeam of each sister's profession crucifix. In these verses Elizabeth reflects on the meaning of her name, "House of the God of Love," as explained on the day of her First Holy Communion, April 19, 1891. It also anticipates themes which emerge in her "Prayer to the Trinity," *written almost a year later.*

There Is This One Who Knows All Mysteries

There is this One who knows all mysteries
And who embraced them from Eternity:
And this same One . . . the Father's *Word* He is—
Splendor, that Word, of His Divinity.
　See that One come, with Love's excess,
　With Charity so urgent! Say:
　"Son of the Father's tenderness—
　God gives us Him on this great day."
　　O Word! may—lifelong now—
　　I listen to You! so
　　Possessed by You, that *how*
　　To love be all I know.
　　　"*Amo Christum.*"

In me, a house that God is living at,
This Jesus Christ, Divine Adorer there,
Takes me to souls, as to the Father: that
Being the double movement of His prayer.
　Co-Savior with my Master, here!—

Whose call to me still drives me on;
For this I ought to disappear—
I lost in Him, with Him as one . . .
   One, Word of Life, with You
   For always! and, above,
   Your virgin *host* anew
   All shining forth with love.
     "Amo Christum."

His sanctuary, I ! He rests in me—
There is the peace one looks for and attains:
In silence, and in deepest mystery,
He's captured me: for ever I'm in chains.
   Ah, to Your ev'ry word to cling,
   Calm in the faith I'm anchored to;
   Adoring You, through everything
   As one who only lives by You!
     Beneath Your splendent Light,
     O Word, by night and day
     May I be now—outright—
     To Your great love, a prey.
      "Amo Christum."

Mother of God, tell me your mystery;
Of how your earthly life was spent: the way—
Right from the time of "Fiat"—how you'd be
Buried in adoration, Mary! Say
   How—in a peace, a silence—you
   (What mystery!) could enter in
   To Deeps that none but you could do—
   Bearing the gift of God within.
     Secure in God's embrace
     Keep me, I ask. In me
     His imprint may He place—
     For wholly Love is he.
      "Amo Christum."

             (P 88, December 1903)

Elizabeth wrote this poem to express her gratitude for Mother Germaine's great kindness throughout her time in Carmel and especially during Elizabeth's terminal illness when she helped to prepare her for death. Elizabeth again uses the language of Mass and offering, with Mother Germaine as "priest."

The Dream of a "Praise of Glory"

I dreamt it was my joy
    (O gentle Shepherdess)
Where Love Itself has Home
    to fête you in the height:
But "Praise of Glory," still
    on earth, can only guess
What was this glimpse she had
    of that abode of Light . . .
Yet: in the Father's house
    (deep down in me I said)
Within that Secret Place,
    the Heart of God, I sense
That, Mother, I on *you*
    in turn might blessings shed!—
This notion flooded me
    with happiness immense.

I never shall forget
    those hours I spent with you:
Your forming of me—for
    the Rendezvous divine;
The plans, together made
    (no words for this will do),
My Spouse would tell me "Come!"—
    I waiting for His sign.
He consecrated you
    to act in this as would
A *priest* in sacrifice:
    you'd offer me and raise

she is the body of Christ consumed by Him!

My being to His love,
  delivered up for good:
To be consumed by Him
  through all my nights and days.

And, Mother—you recall—
  the Stream of Life would flow
Along one channel, you,
  to find its course in me . . .
While I was *in your heart*,
  by faith communing, so
The tides were flooding forth
  to whelm me utterly.
At each new dawn (so deep
  the silence always) you'd
Approach to bring to me
  my Savior and my Lord:
May He express to you
  the love, the gratitude
That in your little child—
  her deeps of heart—are stored.

If, yet, the linen cloth
  God has not willed to tear
That I might shining out
  His hidden Beauty see,
At least I now by faith
  lift up the veil, and there
I live, along with Him
  in His eternity.
Then (deep the mystery!)
  I felt my Master say
That this, my dream of heart,
  was truly to occur.
And for my Mother now
  I do not cease to pray:
"Lord, make her rich in grace"
  in what I ask for her.

My guide, in all I've done
   since coming, has been she:
It's in her arms, then, I
   would fall asleep; to go
To gaze upon that Light
   which beams eternally—
To sing there my *Sanctus*
   that never end shall know!
If "Praise of Glory," here
   on earth, has never found
The words to speak her heart
   in "thank-yous," yet above
A resonating lyre,
   my Mother, by its sound
Will bring you—certainly!
   her sweet refrain of love.

(P 100, 14 September 1906)

Elizabeth had been made Sister Marie-Joseph's "angel," that is, a sister who teaches a postulant the customs of the community. This poem contains many of Elizabeth's favorite themes and, in fact, repeats the first seventeen lines of P 93 which she had written for Guite . . . poetic license!

To One of Her Sisters

How very rich you are—
   dear Sister, do you know?
And have you ever plumbed
   the mighty depth and height?—
A constancy of Love
   (I've come to you to show)
Hovers about your soul
   through every day and night.
Oh, simply look and see
   the Mystery! and how

It works within your heart
   (faith also has its eyes)—
The Holy Spirit's choice,
   His temple are you now:
You are no longer yours,
   and there your greatness lies.
Beneath the touch divine
   in silence live, that He
Imprint Himself in you—
   your Savior's image know,
The likeness pre-ordained
   to be your destiny,
Mysterious! and yet . . .
   our Maker writ it so.
For you become Himself:
   truly, no longer you.
The transformation . . . yes,
   each moment it occurs.
Give thanks, then, to the Lord
   that this He wills to do—
Ah, may your being, deep,
   make adoration hers.
Always believe in love!
   Whatever is the case…
God in your heart's asleep,
   you think? Well, understand
You're not to wake Him up!
   for that's another grace—
That, little sister, then
   He still has you in hand.
An *angel* sent to you,
   I have to come and sing
Before I fly away
   to rest in light above:
And . . . overflowing grace
   to you I'll know to bring

When I shall live up there,
  the Hearth and Home of love.
I'll guide you, ev'ry step
  upon the road ahead,
In spreading over you
  those angel-wings of mine,
That nevermore your feet
may waver as you tread
That then, in everything
  you act by what's Divine.
And, tell me, isn't this
  that thing of precious worth—
Upon a solemn day
  the mission I was giv'n?
Ah! I'll be true to that,
  and even on the earth
I'd like to show'r on you
  all of the gifts of heav'n.
Your *beauty*—that is what
  I'm jealous for! That you
Who bear the title "spouse"
  will measure up to this,
Dear sister, always (that
  I dream that you may do)
Look to the Savior's Cross
  where all your glory is.
Beneath the hand, be calm
  when it shall immolate,
As did your loved one, Christ.
    In ev'ry sorrow He
Stayed as a man of Strength—
  of sovereign peace His state
Up to the last heart's-woe
  —anguish—on Calvary.
Look at and imitate
  this Archetype divine,

Yes, be—whatever comes—
    a copy, really true:
You'll give the Father then
    huge glory, it will shine.
And, you His loving choice,
    He will look after you.

(P 106, July 1906)

One day Elizabeth of the Trinity put a cardboard model of a fortress with drawbridge in the cell of Mother Germaine. Beside the closed door was pasted a cut-out of Our Lady of Lourdes as Janua Caeli *(Gate of Heaven). From one corner of the crenellated tower floated a small standard bearing the words: "Citadel of Pain and Holy Recollection. The dwelling of* Laudem Gloriae *[Praise of Glory, her 'new' name] while awaiting entrance into her Father's house." Beneath the drawbridge was written the following poem in which Elizabeth meditates on Angela of Foligno's words which she first encountered in September 1906 and refers to often in subsequent letters and poems.*

Where Then Did He Dwell But in Suffering?

"Where shall we find the Master!" wrote a saint.
"Where is His house, save in the midst of pain!"
There would I dwell, my Mother and my priest,
To magnify the Cross where He was slain.

But yet I need thee, 'neath thy sheltering wing
To enter this fair palace of my Lord,
This fortress, the strong citadel of God,
Which to the soul doth changeless peace afford.

David hath sung: "Christ's sorrow is immense!"
In this immensity, my home I make;
In sacred silence, self I immolate,
Transformed into love's victim for His sake.

(P 113, 14 September 1906)

Left: As as novice (1902)

Right: Profession, January 1903

Prayer to the Trinity

Elizabeth wrote this profound prayer on the Feast of Mary's Presentation in the Temple after renewing her vows at the end of an eight-day community retreat preached by Father Pierre-Henri Fages, O.P., on the theme of the Mystery of the Incarnation. Sister Thérèse of Lisieux's Act of Oblation[1] and St. Catherine of Siena's O Eternal Trinity,[2] both of which Elizabeth loved, are echoed in this prayer; nonetheless, it is uniquely her own. The prayer encapsulates Elizabeth's Trinitarian spirituality and has an almost sacramental character, insofar as it is a prayer for prayer and effects what it signifies. Elizabeth immerses herself in the mystery of God as Trinity, her "Three." Surrendering herself completely to Father, Son and Spirit, she invites them to take complete possession of her, transforming her into "another humanity," Christ. The church recognizes the deep spirituality of Elizabeth's Prayer to the Trinity *by citing the first paragraph in the* Catechism of the Catholic Church, *n. 260, as the culmination of the section on the Trinity.*

O my God, Trinity Whom I adore; help me to forget myself entirely that I may be established in You as still and as peaceful as if my soul were already in eternity. May nothing trouble my peace or make me leave you, O my Unchanging One, but may each minute carry me further into the depths of Your mystery. Give peace to my soul, make it Your heaven, Your beloved dwelling and Your resting place. May I never leave You there alone but be wholly present, my faith wholly vigilant, wholly adoring and wholly surrendered to Your creative action.

---

1. Clarke, *Story of a Soul: The Autobiography of St. Thérèse of Lisieux: A New Translation From The Original Manuscripts* (Washington: ICS Publications, 1975), 276–7.

2. *The Divine Office: The Liturgy of the Hours According to the Roman Rite* (London-Glasgow: Collins, 2001), vol. II, 124*.

O My beloved Christ, crucified by love, I wish to be a bride for Your Heart; I wish to cover You with glory; I wish to love You . . . even unto death! But I feel my weakness, and I ask You to "clothe me with yourself," to identify my soul with all the movements of Your Soul, to overwhelm me, to possess me, to substitute Yourself for me that my life may be but a radiance of Your Life. Come into me as Adorer, as Restorer, as Savior.

Eternal Word, Word of my God, I want to spend my life in listening to You, to become wholly teachable that I may learn all from You. Then, through all nights, all voids, all helplessness, I want to gaze on You and always remain in Your great light. O my beloved Star, so fascinate me that I may not withdraw from Your radiance.

Consuming Fire, Spirit of Love, "come upon me," and create in my soul a kind of incarnation of the Word: that I may be another humanity for Him in which He can renew His whole Mystery. And You, O Father, bend lovingly over Your poor little creature; "cover her with Your shadow," seeing in her only the "Beloved in whom You are well pleased."

My Three, my All, my Beatitude, infinite Solitude, Immensity in which I lose myself, I surrender myself to You as Your prey. Bury Yourself in me that I may bury myself in You until I depart to contemplate in Your light the abyss of Your greatness.

Composed November 21, 1906
Feast of Mary's Presentation in the Temple

Heaven in Faith

Such was the importance of Elizabeth's new name, "Praise of Glory," which she discovered in 1904, that she devotes two of her most significant writings to it, composed in August 1906 when she was enduring terrible physical suffering. The first account concludes "Heaven in Faith," a retreat written as a "Last Testament," for her beloved sister, Guite. The second, "Last Retreat of the 'Praise of Glory'," was written at the request of Mother Germaine when Elizabeth, knowing she was dying, made a final retreat, a "novitiate for heaven" (L 306.) These "portraits" of a "Praise of Glory" are the culmination of years of prayer and self-giving and provide an interpretive guide for understanding this personal vocation which she wanted others to share. They are particularly fascinating as they are written against the background of eternity: Elizabeth knew they would be her "last words," which gives them a unique power.

A "Praise of Glory"

Written to console and encourage her sister, Guite, this is a beautiful, lyrical meditation on the meaning of the vocation of a "Praise of Glory."

Heaven in Faith

We have been predestined by the decree of Him who works all things according to the counsel of His will, so that we may be the praise of His glory.

It is St. Paul who tells us this, St. Paul who was instructed by God Himself. How do we realize this great dream of the Heart of our God, this immutable will for our souls? In a word, how do we correspond to our vocation and become perfect "Praises of Glory of the Most Holy Trinity"?

In Heaven each soul is a praise of glory of the Father, the Word, and the Holy Spirit, for each soul is established in pure love and "lives no longer its own life, but the life of God." Then it knows Him, St. Paul says, as it is known by Him. In other words, "its intellect is the intellect of God, its will the will of God, its love the very love of God. In reality it is the Spirit of love and of strength who transforms the soul, for to Him it has been given to supply what is lacking to the soul," as St. Paul says again, "He works in it this glorious transformation." St. John of the Cross affirms that "the soul surrendered to love, through the strength of the Holy Spirit, is not far from being raised to the degree of which we have just spoken," even here below! This is what I call a perfect "Praise of Glory"!

A "Praise of Glory" is a soul that lives in God, that loves Him with a pure and disinterested love, without seeking itself in the sweetness of this love; that loves Him beyond all His gifts and even though it would not have received anything from Him, it desires the good of the Object thus loved. Now how do we effectively desire and will good to God if not in accomplishing His will since this will orders everything for His greater glory? Thus, the soul must surrender itself to this will completely, passionately, so as to will nothing else but what God wills.

A "Praise of Glory" is a soul of silence that remains like a lyre under the mysterious touch of the Holy Spirit that He may draw from it divine harmonies; it knows that suffering is a string that produces still more beautiful sounds; so it loves to see this string on its instrument that it may more delightfully move the Heart of its God.

A "Praise of Glory" is a soul that gazes on God in faith and simplicity; it is a reflector of all that He is; it is like a bottomless abyss into which He can flow and expand; it is also like a crystal through which He can radiate and contemplate all His perfections and His own splendor. A soul which thus permits the divine Being to satisfy in itself His need to communicate "all that He is and all that He has," is in reality the praise of glory of all His gifts.

Finally, a "Praise of Glory" is one who is always giving thanks. Each of her acts, her movements, her thoughts, her aspirations, at the same time that they are rooting her more deeply in love, are like an echo of the eternal *Sanctus*.

In the Heaven of glory the blessed have no rest "day or night, saying: Holy, holy, holy is the Lord God Almighty. . . . They fall down and worship Him who lives forever and ever."

In the heaven of her soul, the "Praise of glory" has already begun her work of eternity. Her song is uninterrupted, for she is under the action of the Holy Spirit who effects everything in her; and although she is not always aware of it, for the weakness of nature does not allow her to be established in God without distractions, she always sings, she always adores, for she has, so to speak, wholly passed into praise and love in her passion for the glory of her God. In the heaven of our soul let us be praises of glory of the Holy Trinity, praises of love of our Immaculate Mother. One day the veil will fall, we will be introduced into the eternal courts, and there we will sing in the bosom of infinite Love. And God will give us "the new name promised to the Victor." What will it be?

LAUDEM GLORIAE

The Last Retreat of the "Praise of Glory"

This is a much stronger meditation on the vocation of a "Praise of Glory," demanding in its asceticism and exalted in its goals. Elizabeth made this retreat over a period of sixteen days and these notes on what was, literally, her Last Retreat, her direct preparation for eternity, are a precious insight into her innermost being as she knowingly approaches death.

The First Day

The first stark exclamation plunges the reader into the heart of St. John of the Cross's "Nada, nada, nada." The unknowing which is a most potent form of knowing is the true "song of the Praise of Glory!"

"*Nescivi!*" "I no longer knew anything" (Sg 6:11). So sings the bride of the *Canticles* after having been brought into the inner cellar. That, it seems to me, should be the song of a "Praise of Glory" on the first day of her retreat, when the Master makes her sound the depths of the abyss, that she may learn to fulfill the office which will be hers in eternity and which she ought to perform in time, which is eternity begun, but also in progress. "*Nescivi!*" I know nothing, I desire nothing, except to "know Christ and the power of His resurrection and the sharing of his sufferings by becoming like Him in his death" (Phil 3:10). "Those whom He foreknew He also predestined to be conformed to the image of His divine Son" (Rom 8:29), the One crucified by love. When I become identified with this Divine Exemplar, dwelling wholly in Him and He in me, I shall fulfill my eternal vocation, the one for which God has chosen me in Him "*in principio*," "in the beginning" which I shall fill "*in aeternum*," "in eternity," when, in the bosom of the Trinity, I will be the ceaseless "Praise of His Glory."

and live

"No one has ever seen God. It is God the only Son, who is close to the Father's heart, who has made Him known" (Jn 1:18). One can add that no one, except Our Lady, has penetrated the depths of the mystery of Christ. St. Paul often speaks of the "understanding" (Eph 3:4) which he had received, yet all the saints dwell in shadow when compared with Our Lady's light! The secret which she treasured and pondered in her heart is inexpressible: no tongue can tell or pen describe it!

This Mother of Grace will form my soul so that her little child may be a living, striking image of her "Firstborn" (Col 1:15), the Son of the Eternal Father, He who was the perfect praise of His Father's glory.

The Second Day

Elizabeth writes of full, unifying self-possession, of singleness of purpose. This is the "silence," by which the soul gives herself to God; it is both the means and end of the spiritual journey.

"My soul is continually in my hands" (Ps 119:109, KJV). This was the song of my Master's soul and that is why in the midst of all His anguish, He remained the Calm and Strong One. "My soul is continually in my hands." What does this mean if not that full self-possession in the presence of the Peaceful One?

There is another of Christ's songs which I would like to repeat unceasingly: "O my strength, I will watch for you" (Ps 59:9). My *Rule* tells me: "In silence will be your strength." Keeping your strength for the Lord, therefore, is to unify the whole of one's being by means of interior silence; it means collecting all our powers in order to occupy them in the sole exercise of love; it means having the "simple eye" which allows the light of God to enlighten us.

A soul which argues with itself, which is preoccupied with its feelings, pursuing useless thoughts and desires, scatters its forces, for it is not totally ordered to God. Its lyre is not in tune and when the Divine Master touches it, He is not able to produce divine harmonies. It is still too human and discordant.

The soul which keeps anything for itself in its interior kingdom is not "enclosed" in God and is not able to be a perfect "Praise of Glory"; it is not fit to sing the "*canticum magnum,*" the "great canticle of praise," uninterruptedly because unity does not reign within. So, instead of persevering in praise, in simplicity, through everything, it is ceaselessly obliged to adjust the strings of its instrument which are all a little out of tune.

How necessary is this beautiful interior unity for the soul who wants to live, here below, the life of the Blessed, that is, of simple beings, of spirits. Is not this what the Master wanted to teach Mary Magdalene when He spoke to her of the "*Unum necessarium,*" the "One thing necessary" (see Lk 10:42)? How well that great saint understood! Through the light of faith, she recognized God under the veil of His humanity and, in the silence, in the unity of her powers, she "listened to what He was saying" (Lk 10:39) and was, therefore, able to sing, "My soul is in my hands," and also the little word: "*Nescivi!*"

Yes, she knew nothing but Him; whatever noise and excitement surrounded her, "*Nescivi!*" She could be accused of: "*Nescivi!*" Neither concern for her honor nor exterior things could draw her out of her sacred silence.

It is the same for the soul that has entered into the fortress of holy recollection; the eye of the soul, looking with the clarity of faith, discovers God present, living within; for His part, He is so present to her in her beautiful simplicity, that He guards her with jealous care. Then, whatever disturbances there may be without and whatever tempests within; however her honor may be wounded: "*Nescivi!*" God may hide Himself; He may withdraw His sensible graces, "*Nescivi!*" She cries out: "For his sake I have suffered the loss of all things" (Phil 3:8)! From now on the Divine Master is free, free to flow into her, to give Himself to her according to His measure, and the soul, thus simplified, unified, becomes the throne of the Unchanging One, because unity is the throne of the Blessed Trinity.

The Third Day

Elizabeth takes up her favorite theme of being predestined to be "Praise of His Glory," which is our present and ultimate destiny.

"In Christ we have also obtained an inheritance, having been destined according to the purpose of Him who accomplishes all things according to His counsel and will, so that we, who were the first to set our hope on Christ, might live for the praise of His glory" (Eph 1:11–12).

It is St. Paul who makes known to us this divine election; St. Paul, who penetrated so deeply the secret hidden within the Heart of God. Let us listen now to him who throws light on the vocation to which we are all called. "God," he says, "chose us in Christ before the foundation of the world to be holy and blameless before Him in love" (Eph 1:4). If I compare these two explanations of the divine plan, I conclude from them that in order to worthily fulfill my office of *Laudem gloriae*, "Praise of Glory," I must keep myself, whatever happens, in the presence of God: and even more than that, the Apostle tells us, "*in charitate*," that is to say in God, "*Deus charitas est*," and it is contact with the Divine Being which makes me "holy and blameless" in His eyes.

I apply this to the beautiful virtue of simplicity, "which gives to the soul the repose of the abyss," that is, rest in God, the unfathomable abyss, prelude and echo of the eternal Sabbath of which St. Paul speaks: "We who have believed enter that rest" (Heb 4:3). Glorified souls have this rest in the abyss because they contemplate God in the simplicity of His essence. "They will know fully even as they have been fully known" (see 1 Cor 13:12); that is, by intuitive vision, and that is why they are "transformed into the same image from one degree of glory to another; for this comes from the Lord, the Spirit" (2 Cor 3:18). Then they are a ceaseless praise of glory to the Divine Being, who contemplates His own splendor in them.

I believe that we would give immense joy to the Heart of God by imitating, in the heaven of our soul, this occupation of the blessed, clinging to Him by this simple contemplation which resembles the state of innocence in which man was created. God "created humankind in our image, according to our likeness" (Gn 1:26). Such was the plan of the Creator: to be able to contemplate Himself in His creature, that He might see all His perfections and all His beauty reflected through him as through a pure and flawless crystal. Is not that a kind of extension of His own glory?

The soul, by the simplicity of the gaze which it fixes upon its Divine Object, finds itself separated from everything around it, and separated, above all, from itself. From now on, it is resplendent with the "light of the knowledge of the glory of God" (2 Cor 4:6), because it allows the Divine Being to be reflected in it. Such a soul is truly the "Praise of Glory" of all His gifts; throughout everything, even amidst the most mundane activities, it sings "the *canticum novum*" (Rev 14:3), and this new song thrills God to the very depths of His being. . . .

The Fourth Day

Faith is the light which is indispensable for inner unity: faith in God's love which is the deepest source of our joy.

Yesterday, St. Paul raised the veil a little so that I could catch a glimpse "of the inheritance of the saints in the light" (Col 1:12) that I might see how they employ themselves, and try, as far as possible, to conform my life to theirs, and fulfill my vocation of *Laudem Gloriae*.

Today, it is St. John who partly opens the "ancient doors" (Ps 24:9) for me, that my soul may rest in "Jerusalem the holy, the sweet vision of peace"![1] First of all, he tells me that, "the city has no need of sun, or moon to shine on it, for the glory of God is its light, and its lamp is the Lamb" (Rev 21:23). . . .

Here faith, the beautiful light of faith, appears to me. It alone enlightens me and brings me to the Bridegroom. The psalmist sings that, "He made darkness his covering around Him" (Ps 18:11), but then seems to contradict himself by saying that He is "wrapped in light as with a garment" (Ps 104:2). This apparent contradiction appears to mean that I ought to plunge into the sacred darkness, keeping all my powers in darkness and emptiness; then I shall meet my Master, and the light in which He is "wrapped . . . as with a garment" will envelop me too, for He wishes His bride to be luminous with His light, and with His light alone, "which is the glory of God" (see Rev 21:11).

It is said of Moses that, "by faith he . . . persevered as though he saw him who is invisible" (Heb 11:27). Such should be the attitude of a "Praise of Glory" who desires to persevere in her hymn of thanksgiving whatever happens; to be enduring in her faith, as if she had seen Him who is the Invisible One; enduring in her faith in His "exceeding love"! "We have known and believe the love that God has for us" (1 Jn 4:16).

"Faith is the assurance of things hoped for, the conviction of things not seen" (Heb 11:1). What does it matter to the soul who is so recollected in the light created by this word, whether it feels or does not feel; whether it is in darkness or in light; whether it enjoys or does not enjoy? It experiences a kind of embarrassment in making a distinction between such things, and deeply despising itself for such want of love, turns to its Master for deliverance! "It exalts Him on the highest summit of the mountain of its heart," above the sweetness and consolations which flow from Him, having resolved to transcend everything in order to be united with Him whom it loves.

---

1. From the Office of the Dedication of a Church, in Elizabeth's day.

To this soul, this unshakable believer in the God of Love, may be addressed the words of the Prince of the Apostles, "Even though you do not see Him now, you believe in Him and rejoice with an indescribable and glorious joy" (1 Pt 1:8).

The Fifth Day

St. John of the Cross's image of the "holy fortress" of recollection recurs frequently: nothing can draw her away from God. The soul longs to be conformed to redeem other souls and thus glories in the cross of Christ.

"I looked, and there was a great multitude that no one could count. . . .": those who have come out of the great tribulation (Rev 7:9; 14–17).

All these elect souls, palms in hand, bathed in the light of God, must needs have first passed through "great tribulation" and known the sorrow "great as the sea" sung by the prophet. Before contemplating the glory of the Lord "face to face," they have shared in the annihilation of His Christ: before being "transformed from glory to glory into the image of the divine" they have been conformed to that of the Word Incarnate, crucified by love.

The soul that longs to serve God day and night in His temple, in the inner sanctuary of which St. Paul speaks when he says: "God's temple is holy, and you are that temple" (1 Cor 3:17). Such a soul must be resolved to share in the Passion of the Master. It is a ransom which in its turn will ransom other souls, and will then sing on its lyre: "May I never boast . . ." (Gal 6:14); "I have been crucified with Christ" (Gal 2:19). And again: "in my flesh I am completing what is lacking in Christ's afflictions . . ." (Col 1:24). "At your right hand stands the queen" (Ps 45:9). Such is the attitude of this soul; it walks on the road to Calvary at the right hand of her crucified, crushed, humbled King who is always so strong, so calm, so full of majesty, going to His passion "to the praise of His glorious grace" (Eph 1:6).

He desires His bride to join in His work of redemption, and the way of sorrow which she treads seems to her the way of beatitude, not only because it leads there, but also because her holy Master makes her understand that she must pass beyond the bitterness of suffering, to find her rest in it, as He did.

Then she can "serve God day and night in His temple." Neither interior nor exterior trials can make her leave the fortress in which He has enclosed her. She no longer thirsts or hungers, for in spite of her overwhelming longings for heaven she is satisfied with the food that was her Master's, the will of the Father. She no longer feels the "sun fall on her," that is, she does not suffer from suffering, and the "Lamb . . . can lead her to the fountains of the waters of life," where He wills, as He wills, for she looks not at the path on which she is walking, but at the Shepherd who guides her.

God, bending down toward this soul, His adopted daughter who so closely resembles His Son, "the firstborn of all creation" (Col 1:15), recognizes it as one whom He has predestined, called and justified; and His Fatherly heart thrills at the thought of perfecting His work, that is, glorifying her by transferring her to His kingdom, there to sing through endless ages "the praise of His glory!"

The Sixth Day

Immersed in Scripture, Elizabeth's word is God's own. At the end of her life, the "Apocalypse" resonates with fresh meaning. This exalted vision, however, is only achieved through total death to self. The tone of the "Last Retreat" intensifies as Elizabeth faces this stark reality.

"Then I looked, and there was the Lamb, standing on Mount Zion! And with Him were one hundred and forty-four thousand who had His name and his Father's name written on their foreheads. And I heard a voice from heaven like the sound of many waters and like the sound of loud thunder; the voice I heard was like the sound of harpists playing on their harps, and they sang a new song before the throne.... No one could learn that song except the one hundred and forty-four thousand . . . for they are virgins; these follow the Lamb wherever He goes . . ." (Rev 14:1–4).

There are some who are as pure as light and who, even here on earth belong to this generation; they already bear the name of the Lamb and of the Father written on their foreheads. "The name of the Lamb," by their resemblance and conformity with Him whom St. John called, "Faithful and True," whom He shows us clothed in a robe stained with blood. These Christians are also faithful and true, and their robes are stained with the blood of their perpetual immolation. "The name of the Father," because He radiates the beauty of His perfection in them, all His divine attributes being reflected in such souls, which are like so many strings of an instrument, vibrating and singing the *"Canticum Novum."*

"They follow the Lamb wherever He goes," not only by the broad and easy roads but by thorny paths, among the brambles by the way. They are virgins, that is, free, set apart, detached; "free from all except their love," separated from all, above all from self, detached from all, both in the supernatural and natural order. What a going out from self does this imply! What a death! As St. Paul says: "I die every day!" (1 Cor 15:31).

The great saint wrote to the Colossians: "You have died, and your life is hidden with Christ in God" (Col 3:3). This is the condition: we must be *dead*; otherwise, we may be hidden in God at certain times, but we do not habitually *live* in this Divine Being, because our feelings, our self-seeking and the rest, draw us forth from Him. . . .

O, blessed death in God! O, sweet and delightful loss of self within Him whom we love! Henceforth the creature can say: "I have been crucified with Christ; and it is no longer I who live, but it is Christ who lives in me. And the life I now live in the flesh I live by faith in the Son of God, who loved me and gave Himself for me" (Gal 2:19–20).

The Seventh Day

Meditating on Psalm 18, the "Praise of Glory," contemplates God through everything. "Night," all the human weaknesses and suffering which we fear may block our way, astonishingly can be messages of glory.

"*Caeli enarrant gloriam Dei*," "The heavens are telling the glory of God" (Ps 19:1). This is what the heavens declare: "the glory of God."

Since my soul is a heaven wherein I dwell, while awaiting the heavenly Jerusalem, this heaven, too, must sing the glory of the Eternal: nothing but the glory of the Eternal. "Day to day pours forth speech" (Ps 19:2). All the light, the communications from God to my soul, are this "day" which "pours forth speech" of His glory to "the day." "The commandment of the Lord is clear, enlightening the eyes" (Ps 19:8), sings the psalmist. Consequently, my fidelity to all His commandments and interior promptings causes me to live in the light; it is also the "speech" which "pours forth" His glory. But what a sweet mystery! "Look to Him, and be radiant!" (Ps 34:5). The soul which, by its far-seeing inner gaze, contemplates God with a simplicity that separates it from all else, is "radiant"; it is a day that passes on the "speech" today of His glory.

"Night to night declares knowledge" (Ps 19:2). How consoling this is! My helplessness, my dislikes, my ignorance, my very faults themselves declare the glory of the Eternal! And my sufferings of body and soul "tell the glory of God!"

"What shall I return to the Lord for all His bounty to me? I will lift up the cup of salvation and call on the name of the Lord" (Ps 116:12–13). If I take this cup, crimsoned with the blood of my Master, and in joyous thanksgiving mingle my own blood with that of the sacred Victim who gives it a share of His own infinity, it may bring wonderful glory to the Father; then my suffering is a "speech" which transmits the glory of the Eternal.

There, in the soul which "declares His glory"; "He has set a tent for the sun." The Sun is the Word, the Bridegroom. If He finds my soul empty of all that is not included in the two words, His love, His glory, He chooses it for His "wedding canopy." He rushes in with joy, "like a strong man running its course" and I cannot "escape His heat." This is the consuming fire (Heb 12:29) which will work that blessed transformation spoken of by St. John of the Cross. "Each of them *seems to be the other*, and they are both but one": a "Praise of Glory" of the Father.

The Eighth Day

Old and New Testament, Isaiah and Apocalypse, unite in a hymn to God's holiness. Elizabeth is enraptured by the thought of transcending self in complete adoration of God.

"Day and night without ceasing they sing, 'Holy, holy, holy, the Lord God the Almighty, who was and is and is to come.' And . . . the twenty-four elders fall before the one who is seated on the throne and worship the one who lives for ever and ever; they cast their crowns before the throne, singing, 'You are worthy, our Lord and God, to receive glory and honor and power' " (Rev 4:8, 10–11).

How can I imitate within the heaven of my soul the ceaseless work of the blessed in the heaven of glory? How can I maintain this constant praise, this uninterrupted adoration? St. Paul enlightens me when he writes to his disciples, praying that: "the Father . . . may grant that you may be strengthened in your inner being with power through his Spirit, and that Christ may dwell in your hearts through faith, as you are being rooted and grounded in love" (Eph 3:14, 16–17).

To be "rooted and grounded in love," it seems to me is the necessary condition for worthily fulfilling the office of *Laudem Gloriae*. The soul that enters into, and dwells in "the deep things of God," and consequently does all "by Him, with Him, in Him," with the purity of intention that gives it a certain resemblance to the one, simple Being, this soul, by its every aspiration, every impulse, every action, however commonplace, becomes more deeply rooted in Him it loves. Everything within it renders homage to the thrice-holy God; it may be called a perpetual *Sanctus*, a perpetual "Praise of Glory."

"They fall . . . and worship . . . they cast their crowns before the throne."

First of all, the soul should "fall down," should plunge into the abyss of its own nothingness, so sinking into it that, according to the beautiful expression of a mystic, "it finds that true peace, perfect and unchanging, which nothing can disturb, for it has cast itself so low that no one will look for it." Then, it can *adore*!

Adoration! Ah, that is a word which comes from heaven. It seems to me that it can be defined as the ecstasy of love; love overwhelmed by the beauty, strength, the immense grandeur of Him it loves. It falls into a kind of swoon, into a profound and deep silence, that silence of which David spoke when he cried: "Silence is your praise!" (see Ps 65:1). Yes! That is the most perfect praise, for it is sung eternally in the bosom of the tranquil Trinity; it is also the "final effort of the soul that overflows and can no longer speak. . . ."

It knows that He whom it adores possesses in Himself all happiness, all glory, and "casting its crown" before Him, as do the blessed, it despises self, loses sight of self, and finds its beatitude in Him whom it adores, whatever its sufferings or grief, for it has gone out of itself and passed into Another. In this attitude of adoration, the soul "resembles the wells," spoken of by St. John of the Cross, which receive "the waters that flow from Lebanon";[2] so that those who look on it can exclaim: "There is a river whose streams make glad the city of God" (Ps 46:4).

The Ninth Day

Contemplation of God's holiness leads to an unquenchable desire for personal holiness, only achieved when we die to self in every way. Elizabeth writes this retreat while enduring excruciating suffering: she lives what she speaks.

"You shall be holy, for I the Lord your God am holy" (Lev 19:2). Who is He who can give such a command? He Himself revealed His name, the name proper to Him, which He alone possesses. "God said to Moses: 'I Am Who Am' " (Ex 3:14); the one who lives, the principle of all living beings. "In Him we live and move and have our being" (Acts 17:28).

"Be holy for I am holy." It seems to me that this is the wish expressed on the day of creation when God said: "Let us make humankind in our image, according to our likeness" (Gn 1:26). The Creator's idea has always been to associate and to identify His creature with Himself.

St. Peter writes that we are to be made "participants of the divine nature" (2 Pt 1:4). St. Paul recommends us to "hold our first confidence firm to the end," which He has given us (Heb 3:14); and the disciple of love tells us: "We are God's children now; what we will be has not yet been revealed. What we do know is this: when He is revealed, we will be like Him, for we will see Him as He is. And all who have this hope in Him purify themselves, just as He is pure" (1 Jn 3:2–3).

To be holy, as God is holy, is the measure for the children of His love. Has not the Master said: "Be perfect, therefore, as your heavenly Father is perfect" (Mt 5:48)? God said

---

2. *The Living Flame of Love,* 3:7, in Kavanaugh and Rodriguez, 613.

to Abraham: "Walk in my presence and be perfect" (see Gn 17:1). This then is the means by which to attain the perfection that our Heavenly Father asks of us.

St. Paul, after having immersed himself in the divine counsels, reveals this to us clearly in the words: "He chose us in Christ before the foundation of the world to be holy and blameless before Him in love. He destined us for adoption as His children through Jesus Christ" (Eph 1:4–5). I seek light from the same saint in order to walk unerringly on this magnificent way of the presence of God, on which the soul travels "alone with the One," led by the help of His "right hand" (Ps 20:6), "under His wings . . . you will not fear the terror of the night, or the arrow that flies by day, or the pestilence that stalks in darkness, or the destruction that wastes at noonday" (Ps 91:4–6).

"Put away your former way of life, your old self . . . to clothe yourselves with the new self, created according to the likeness of God in true righteousness and holiness" (Eph 4:22–24). This is the path traced out for us. We have but to deny ourselves, to die to self, to lose sight of self. This seems to be what the Master means when He says: "If any want to become my followers, let them deny themselves and take up their cross" (Mt 16:24). . . .

The Tenth Day

The soul longs to live the perfection of God, the wholeness which unites time, place, and person in an "eternal now." Always realistic, Elizabeth knows that only the "sleep" of the "noise within," the overcoming of our distracting passions, can bring spiritual serenity.

"Be perfect, therefore, as your heavenly Father is perfect" (Mt 5:48). When my Master makes me hear this sentence in the depths of my soul, I realize that He is asking me to live, like the Father, in an *eternal present*, with no past, no future, but, in unity of being, solely in the *eternal present*.

What is this present? David tells me: "They shall adore Him continually for His own sake." This is the "eternal present" in which a "Praise of Glory" should abide. But if her attitude of adorer is to be real, so that she can sing: "I will awake the dawn," she must also be able to say: "For His sake I have suffered the loss of all things" (Phil 3:8), that is, for His sake, that I may adore Him always, I have isolated, separated, stripped myself of all things with regard to the natural and the supernatural gifts of God. For unless a soul has destroyed and become emancipated from self, it must of necessity, at certain times, be commonplace and natural, which is unworthy of a child of God, a bride of Christ and a temple of the Holy Spirit.

As a protection against living according to nature, the soul must have a lively faith, and must keep its eyes fixed upon the Master; then it can say: "I will walk with integrity of heart within my house" (Ps 101:3). It will adore God for His own sake, and will dwell like Him, as He does, by His example, in the "eternal present" in which He lives.

"Be perfect, therefore, as your heavenly Father is perfect." "God," says St. Denis, "is *the great solitary*." My Master bids me imitate this perfection, to render Him homage by living in strict solitude. The Divinity dwells in eternal and profound solitude; He cares for the needs of His creature without in any way leaving it, for He never goes out from Himself, and this solitude is nothing but His Divinity.

In order to guard against being withdrawn from this holy interior silence I must keep myself always in the same state, the same isolation, the same retirement, the same detachment. If my desires, my fears, my joys, or my sorrows, if all the impulses coming from these four passions are not completely subjected to God, I shall not be solitary: there will be turmoil within me. Therefore, calm, the slumber of the powers, the unity of the whole being are needed. "Listen, O daughter, lend your ear: forget your people and your father's house, and the King shall greatly desire your beauty" (Ps 45:10–11).

This injunction is a call to keep silence: "Consider . . . incline your ear." But in order to listen we must forget our "father's house," that is, whatever pertains to the natural life, of which the apostle says: "If you live according to the flesh, you will die" (Rom 8:13).

To forget our people is more difficult, for this "people" is that world which is, as it were, a part of ourselves; it includes our feelings, memories, impressions, etc., in a word, the *self*. We must forget it, give it up, and when the soul has broken with it and is wholly delivered from all it means, "the King will desire your beauty," for beauty is *unity*, at least as regards divine beauty.

The Eleventh Day

Solitude enables the soul to listen attentively to the voice of God. His word will complete the stripping of the soul which will then resemble the Trinity.

"He brought me out into a broad place . . . because He delighted in me" (Ps 18:19). The Creator, seeing that silence reigns within His creature who is deeply recollected in her interior solitude, greatly desires her beauty. He leads her into that immense and infinite solitude, into that "broad space" of which the psalmist sings, which is His very Self: "I will come praising the mighty deeds of the Lord God" (Ps 71:16). . . .

This word will finish the work of stripping the soul, for it has the particular characteristic that it creates what it intends, provided that the soul yields its consent.

It is not enough, however, just to listen to this word. The soul must also keep the word, and by this keeping be sanctified in the truth, according to the will of the Divine Master: "Sanctify them in the truth; your word is truth" (Jn 17:17). To those who keep His word He had promised: "My Father will love them, and we will come to them and make our home *with them*" (Jn 14:23).

The whole Blessed Trinity dwells within the soul which loves them "in truth," that is, by keeping their word. And when this soul realizes what riches it possesses, whatever natural or supernatural joy it feels only induces it to enter within itself to enjoy the substantial good it owns, which is nothing else but God Himself. So that St. John of the Cross declares: "It has a certain resemblance to the Divinity."[3]

"Be perfect, as your Father in heaven is perfect." St. Paul tells me that He "accomplishes all things according to his counsel and will" (Eph 1:11), and my Master asks me again to render Him homage in this manner: "To do all things according to my counsel and will"; never to let myself be led by my impressions, by the first impulses of nature, but to control myself by my will. For this will to be free, it must be "enshrined within the will of God"; then shall I be "led by the Spirit of God" (Rom 8:14). All that I do will partake of the divine, the eternal, and, like Him who changes not, I shall dwell here on earth in an *eternal present*.

The Twelfth Day

We become holy with God's holiness; this is our baptismal calling. The heaven of our soul then provides a fitting dwelling for "the Three."

"*Verbum caro factum est, et habitavit in nobis.*" "The Word became flesh and lived among us" (Jn 1:14). God has said: "Be holy, because I the Lord your God am holy," but He remained inaccessible and hidden. The creature, therefore, needed Him to descend to it; to live its life, so that, setting its feet in His footsteps it would be able to ascend to Him, becoming holy with His holiness.

---

3. *The Spiritual Canticle* 39:4, 6, *The Collected Works of St. John of the Cross*, 558–9.

"For their sakes I sanctify myself, so that they also may be sanctified in truth" (Jn 17:19). I find myself in the presence of "a mystery that has been hidden throughout the ages and generations . . . this mystery which is Christ in you, the hope of glory" (Col 1:26–27), says St. Paul, adding that the mystery had been manifested to him. It is, then, from this great Apostle that I shall learn how I may possess this wisdom "which surpasses all knowledge, the charity of Jesus Christ" (see Eph 3:19).

First of all, he tells me: "He is my peace," that "through Him both of us have access in one Spirit to the Father" (Eph 2:18). "For in Him all the fullness of God was pleased to dwell, and through Him God was pleased to reconcile to Himself all things, whether on earth or in heaven, by making peace through the blood of His cross" (Col 1:19–20). "And you have come to fullness in Him," continues the Apostle, "You were buried with Him in baptism, you were also raised with Him through faith in God. . . . God made you alive together with Him, when He forgave us all our trespasses, erasing the record that stood against us with its legal demands. He set this aside, nailing it to the cross. He disarmed the rulers and authorities and made a public example of them, triumphing over them in it . . ." (Col 2:10, 12–15) "to present you holy and blameless and irreproachable before Him" (Col 1:22). This is the work of Christ as regards every soul of good will and it is the work which the Father, in His immense, His "exceeding love" urges Him to do for me.

He wants to be my peace, so that nothing can distract my attention nor draw me out of the invincible fortress of holy recollection. It is there that He will give me "access to the Father," and will keep me as still and peaceful in His presence as if my soul were already in eternity. By the blood of the cross He will make peace in my little heaven, that it may be indeed the place of repose of the Holy Trinity. . . . He will fill me with Himself; He will absorb me into Himself, making me live with Him by His life; "*Mihi vivere Christus est.*" "For me living is Christ" (Phil 1:21).

And if I fall at every moment, in confident faith I will ask Him to help me up again. I know that He will forgive me and, with jealous care, cancel out everything. Even more than that, He will strip me; will deliver me from my miseries, from everything that is an obstacle to the divine action upon me. He will draw my powers to Him and make them captive, triumphing over them in Himself. Then I shall have passed completely into Him and shall be able to say: "I no longer live, it is Christ Jesus who lives in me," and I shall be "holy, blameless, and irreproachable before Him."

The Thirteenth Day

Elizabeth again takes up the clarion call of Pope Pius X's pontificate, to "restore all things in Christ," as a personal challenge, resolving to realize this "divine plan" through rooting herself totally in Christ (see P 89 above).

"*Instaurare omnia in Christo.*" "Restore all things in Christ" (see Eph 1:10). Again it is St. Paul who teaches me. He, who has just immersed himself in the divine counsels, tells me that "God has resolved in Himself to restore all things in Christ."

In order to help me to realize fully this divine plan, the Apostle comes to my aid again, and gives me a rule of life: "As you therefore have received Christ Jesus the Lord, so walk in Him, rooted and built up in Him and established in the faith, as you have been taught, abounding in it with thanksgiving" (Col 2:6–7, KJV).

"To walk in Jesus Christ" seems to me to mean to go out from self, to lose sight of self, to leave self, in order that we may enter more deeply into Him every moment, enter so profoundly as to be "rooted" there, that we may boldly challenge all events with the defiant cry: "Who, then, shall separate us from the love of Christ?" When the soul is so deeply fixed in Him as to be rooted in Him, the divine sap flows freely into it and destroys whatever in its life is trivial, imperfect or unspiritual: "That what is mortal may be swallowed up by life" (2 Cor 5:4). Thus stripped of self and clothed in Jesus Christ, the soul no longer fears assaults from without or difficulties within; far from being an impediment, all such things only serve to root it more firmly in its love for its Master. Throughout everything, despite everything, the soul is ready to "adore Him always for His own sake," because it is free, liberated from self and all else. It can sing with the psalmist: "Though an army encamp against me, my heart shall not fear; though war rise up against me, yet I will be confident. . . . For He will hide me in His shelter in the day of trouble; He will conceal me under the cover of His tent" (Ps 27:3, 5), that is, in Himself. I think this is what St. Paul means when he speaks of being "rooted in Jesus Christ."

Now, what does it mean to be "built up in Him"? The prophet also sings: "He will set me high on a rock. Now my head is lifted up above my enemies all around me" (Ps 27:5–6). I think that this is an image of the soul "built up" in Jesus Christ. He is that rock on which the soul is set high above self, the senses and nature; above consolations and sufferings; above all that is not Him alone! There, with perfect self-possession, it overcomes itself, rising above self and everything else as well.

St. Paul also advises me to "hold firm in faith"; in that faith which never permits the soul to slumber, but keeps it wholly vigilant under its Master's gaze, wholly recollected as it listens to His creative word; in that faith in His "exceeding love," which allows God to fill the soul "with His fullness."

Finally, the Apostle desires that I "grow in Jesus Christ through thanksgiving," for everything should end in this. "Father, I thank you," was the song of Christ's soul, and He wants to hear it echoed in mine. But I think that the "new song" which will best charm and captivate my God is that of a soul detached from all things, delivered from self, one in whom He can reflect all that He is and do all that He wills. Such a soul remains under His touch, as though it were a lyre,

and all His gifts are like so many strings which vibrate to sing
out, day and night, the "praise of His glory"!

The Fourteenth Day

*Elizabeth wants to be conformed to Christ in order to be transformed
into a worthy bride for him. This section contains the most vivid expression of Elizabeth's actual suffering and spiritual identification with
Jesus, expressed in the stark language of his passion: she is on her
deathbed. It is the darkest, most moving part of the "Last Retreat," and
yet she tastes "divine sweetness."*

"I regard everything as loss because of the surpassing value of
knowing Christ Jesus my Lord. For his sake I have suffered the
loss of all things . . . that I may gain Christ and be found in
Him, not having a righteousness of my own that comes from
the law, but one that comes through faith in Christ, the righteousness from God based on faith. I want to know Christ and
the power of His resurrection and the sharing of His sufferings by becoming like Him in His death. . . . Not that I have
already obtained this or have already reached the goal; but I
press on to make it my own, because Christ Jesus has made
me His own. . . . This one thing I do: forgetting what lies
behind and straining forward to what lies ahead, I press on
toward the goal for the prize of the heavenly call of God in
Christ Jesus" (Phil 3:8–10, 12–14).

The Apostle has often revealed the greatness of this vocation: "God has chosen us in Him before the foundation of the
world, that we should be holy and blameless before Him in
love" (see Eph 1:4). "We . . . have been destined according
to the purpose of Him Who accomplishes all things according
to His counsel and will: that we . . . might live for the praise
of His glory" (see Eph 1:11, 12).

How are we to respond to the dignity of our vocation?
This is the secret: *"Mihi vivere Christus est."* "For to me, living

is Christ" (Phil 1:21). *"Vivo enim, jam non ego, vivit vero in me Christu."* "It is no longer I who live, but it is Christ who lives in me" (Gal 2:20). We must be transformed into Jesus Christ, and study this divine model, so that, thoroughly identifying ourselves with Him, we can ceaselessly represent Him before the eyes of His Father.

What were His first words on entering the world? "See, I have come to do your will" (Heb 10:9).

The Divine Master was truth itself in His first oblation; and His life was a consequence of this offering. He delighted in saying: "My food is to do the will of Him that sent me" (Jn 4:34). This should be the food of the bride, and at the same time, the sword that immolates her.

"Abba, Father, for you all things are possible; remove this cup from me; yet, not what I want, but what you want" (Mk 14:36). Then, in joyful peace, she will go to meet all sacrifices with her Master, rejoicing at "having been known" by the Father, since He crucifies her with His Son. By never leaving Him, by keeping in such close contact with Him, she will radiate the secret *power*, which delivers and saves souls. Stripped, set free from self and all things, she will follow her Master to the mountain, to join with Him, in her soul in "prayer to God" (Lk 6:12). Then, still through the divine Adorer, she will, "continually offer a sacrifice of praise to God, that is, the fruit of lips that confess His Name" (Heb 13:15). And she will praise "the might of His awesome deeds, and declare His greatness" (see Ps 145:6).

In the hour of humiliation, of annihilation, she will remember these few words: *"Jesus, autem, tacebat"*; "Jesus suffered in silence" (see Mk 15:5); and she, too, will be silent, "keeping all her strength for the Lord" (see Ps 59:10), the strength which we draw from silence.

When the hour of abandonment, desertion, and anguish comes, the hour that drew forth from Christ the loud cry:

"Why have you forsaken me?" (Mk 15:34) she will remember the prayer: "That they may have my joy made complete in them" (Jn 17:13); and, drinking to the very dregs the chalice prepared by the Father (Jn 18:11), she will find a divine sweetness in its bitterness.

Finally, after having repeated again and again: "I thirst!" thirst to possess you in glory, she will die, exclaiming: "It is finished . . ." (Jn 19:30); "Into your hands I commend my spirit" (Lk 23:46). Then the Father will come to bring her into His inheritance, where "in your light we see light" (Ps 36:9). "Know that the Lord has made His Holy One" wonderful (see Ps 4:3), sang David. Yes, in the case of such a soul, God's holy One is glorified indeed, for He will have destroyed all else to clothe it with Himself, and it will have conformed its life to the words of the Precursor: "He must increase, but I must decrease" (Jn 3:30).

The Fifteenth Day

Jesus has substituted Elizabeth for himself on the cross and given her his mother, Mary, as teacher and guide. The retreat moves from death to glory, as Elizabeth reflects on the Blessed Virgin, "the great Praise of Glory of the Holy Trinity," who will lead her home.

Nearer than all to Jesus Christ, though at the distance which there is between the Infinite and the finite, there is a created being, who was also the great "Praise of Glory" of the Blessed Trinity. She responded fully to the divine vocation of which the Apostle speaks; she was always holy, immaculate, blameless, in the sight of the thrice-holy God.

Her soul is so simple, its movements are so profound, that they cannot be discerned; she seems to reproduce on earth the life of the Divine Being. And she is so transparent, so luminous, that she might be taken for the light itself; yet she is but the mirror of the Sun of justice (*Spaeculum justitae*).

"The Virgin treasured all these things in her heart" (see Lk 2:51). Her whole history can be summed up in these few words. It was within her own heart that she dwelt, and so deeply that no human eye can follow her. . . .

Her humility was so genuine! For she was always self-forgetful, knowing nothing, freed from self, so that she could sing: "The Mighty One has done great things for me; from now on all generations will call me blessed" (Lk 1:49, 48).

This Queen of Virgins is also Queen of Martyrs; it was her heart that was pierced by the sword, for with her everything took place within her soul.

Oh! How beautiful she is to contemplate during her long martyrdom, enveloped in a majesty that radiates both strength and sweetness, for she has learned from the Word Himself how those must suffer whom the Father has chosen as victims; those whom He has elected as associates in the great work of the redemption; whom He has known and "predestined to be conformed to the image of His Son" (Rom 8:29), crucified by love.

She is there, at the foot of the cross; she *stands*, full of strength and courage, and my Master tells me: "*Ecce Mater tua.*" He gives her to me for my Mother! And now that He has returned to His Father, and has substituted me for Himself on the cross, so that "I am completing what is lacking in Christ's afflictions for the sake of His body, that is, the Church" (Col 1:24), the Blessed Virgin is still there, to teach me to suffer as He did, to let me hear the last song of His soul which no one but His Mother could overhear.

When I shall have said my "*consummatum est,*" "It is finished" (Jn 19:30), it will be she again, "*Janua Caeli,*" who will lead me into the eternal courts as she utters the mysterious words: "*Laetatus sum in his quae dicta sunt mihi, in domum Domini ibimus.*" "I was glad when they said to me, 'Let us go to the house of the Lord!' " (Ps 122:1).

all the pryl

The Sixteenth Day

It is fitting that Elizabeth, House of God, should conclude her retreat on what was then the feast of the Dedication of the Churches of Carmel. The scriptural texts she cites are all from the Divine Office for that day. Elizabeth's soul soars, transcending earthly limitations, rising to the limitlessness of the unfathomable Trinity. She leaves us, "trailing clouds of glory," inviting us to follow.

"As a deer longs for flowing streams, so my soul longs for you, O God. My soul thirsts for God, for the living God. When shall I come and behold the face of God?" (Ps 42:1–2).

And yet, "the sparrow finds a home, and the swallow a nest for herself, where she may lay her young" (Ps 84:3); so, while waiting to be taken to the holy city of Jerusalem, "*Beata pacis visio,*" "Blessed vision of peace," *Laudem Gloriae* has found her retreat, her beatitude, her anticipated heaven, where she already begins her life of eternity.

"In God my soul is silent, my deliverance comes from Him. Yes, He is the rock where I find salvation, my citadel, and I shall not be moved! For God alone my soul waits in silence; from him comes my salvation. He alone is my rock and my salvation, my fortress; I shall never be shaken" (Ps 62:1–2).

This is the mystery which my lyre sings of today. My divine Master has said to me, as He did to Zaccheus: "Hurry and come down; for I must stay at your house today" (Lk 19:5). Make haste and descend, but where? Into the innermost depths of my being, after having left self, stripped myself of self, in a word, without self.

"I must stay at your house." It is my Master who expresses this desire, my Master who desires to dwell in me with the Father and His Spirit of love so that I may "have fellowship" with Them (1 Jn 1:3). As St. Paul says, "You are no longer strangers and aliens, but you are citizens with the saints and also members of the household of God" (Eph 2:19).

I think that to belong to the household of God means to live in the bosom of the tranquil Trinity, in my interior abyss, in the invincible fortress of holy recollection described by St. John of the Cross. "My soul longs, indeed it faints for the courts of the Lord" (Ps 84:2).

Such should be the attitude of every soul who enters its interior courts in order to contemplate God and come into close contact with Him. It "indeed faints" in a divine swoon before this all powerful love, this infinite Majesty that dwells within it. It is not that life forsakes it, but rather the soul itself disdains this natural life and withdraws from it. Feeling such life to be unworthy of the soul's rich essence, it dies to this life and flows into its God.

Oh! How beautiful is the creature thus stripped and freed! She is in a state which is disposed to ascend by the steps of her heart, to pass "through the valley of Baca" (Ps 84:6) (that is, from all that is less than God), to the place which is its goal, that "vast space" which is the unfathomable Trinity: "*Immensus Pater, immensus Filius, immensus Spiritus Sanctus.*" "Immense Father, Immense Son, Immense Spirit."[4]

The soul rises, ascending above the senses, above nature, above self. It transcends all joy and all sorrow, and passes through the clouds, never to rest until it has penetrated the *interior* of Him whom it loves, and who will Himself give it the "repose of the abyss." And all that without leaving the "holy fortress." The Divine Master has said to it: "Hurry and come down."

It is also without leaving it, that the soul will live, like the immutable Trinity, in an "eternal present," adoring Him always for Himself and becoming, by an ever more simple and unifying gaze, "the splendor of His glory" (see Heb 1:3), that is, the unceasing "Praise of Glory" of His adorable perfections.

---

4. From the Athanasian Creed, then often recited on Sundays.

Right: "Praise of Glory." Photograph taken in the monastery courtyard at the time of her profession.

Left: Taken around October 4, 1906, a month before her death. This photo shows the ravages of her illness.

Chronology
(1880–1906)

1880

July 18 — Born in military barracks Camp d'Avour, Cher, near Bourges.

July 22 — Baptized Marie Joséphine Elizabeth Catez on the feast of St. Mary Magdalene.

1882

May 9 — Grandmother, Madame Rolland, dies in St. Hilaire, and her grandfather, Commandant Rolland, comes to live with them.

Nov. 1 — The family moves to Dijon.

1883

Feb. 20 — Marguerite/Guite is born.

1885

June 2 — Captain Catez retires from the army, aged 52, because of his poor health.

1887

Jan. 24 — Commandant Rolland dies.

Oct. 2 — Captain Catez, aged 54, dies of a heart attack in Elizabeth's arms.

Madame Catez and her daughters move to Prieur-de-la-Côte-d'Or, near Dijon Carmel.

Elizabeth makes her first confession.

1891

April 19 — First Holy Communion at St. Michael.

Visits Carmel that afternoon; the prioress reveals her name means "House of God."

June 8 — Confirmation at Notre-Dame.

1893

July 25 — First prize for piano at Dijon Conservatory.

1894 — Private vow of perpetual virginity. Feels interior call to "Carmel."

1897	Elizabeth asks her mother's permission to enter Carmel, but Madame Catez refuses. Elizabeth resolves to live her Carmelite vocation "in the world."
1899	
March 4	Mission preached in Dijon until April 2, Easter Sunday.
March 26	Palm Sunday, Madame Catez agrees to Elizabeth entering Carmel when she is 21.
June 20	Elizabeth's first visit to the parlor of Carmel, after her mother's consent.
	Some time in 1899, Elizabeth reads St. Thérèse of Lisieux's *Histoire d'une Âme* (*Story of a Soul*).
1900	
Jan. 23–27	After experiencing a sense of being "indwelt" Elizabeth speaks to Father Vallée, a Dominican.
1901	
August 2	First Friday, Elizabeth enters Carmel and receives the name Sister Marie Elizabeth of the Trinity.
Dec. 8	Elizabeth receives the Carmelite habit. Bishop Albert Leon-Marie Le Nordez presides. Father Vallée preaches.
1902	
Aug.–Sept.	Meets Abbé André Chevignard, Georges' brother, a 23-year-old seminarian.
Oct. 7–14	Community retreat preached by Father Vallée, who cannot understand Elizabeth's state of soul.
Oct. 15	Marguerite marries Georges Chevignard.
Dec. 22	Canonical examination before profession.
	Elizabeth spends time outside enclosure with her mother and sister.
1903	
Jan. 11	Epiphany Sunday, Elizabeth makes her solemn religious profession. Peace returns.
Jan. 21	Feast of St. Agnes, Elizabeth receives the black veil. Second portress, assistant robier.

Some time in 1903 she is diagnosed with Addison's Disease.

1904

Jan. 25   L 191 to Abbé Chevignard in which Elizabeth first sums up her vocation as "Praise of Glory."

March 11   Elizabeth Chevignard is born. (Enters Dijon Carmel, Sister Elizabeth of Jesus, died 1991).

Nov. 12–20 Community retreat preached by Father Pierre-Henri Fages, OP, who focuses on the Annunciation.

Nov. 21   Feast of the Presentation; writes *Prayer to the Trinity*. Found only after her death.

1905

March 8–April 22   Lent: first symptoms of Addison's Disease taking hold. Dispensations from the *Rule*.

April 19   Odette Chevignard is born.

1906

Jan. 1   Elizabeth receives St. Joseph as her patron for the year: "St. Joseph is the patron of a happy death, he will come to lead me to the Father."

Jan. 15–23 Community retreat preached by Father Rollin, SJ. Lent: "I want to know Christ and the power of His resurrection and the sharing of His sufferings by becoming like Him in His death" (Phil 3:10).

About March 19   Elizabeth is moved (permanently) to the infirmary.

April 8   Palm Sunday, Elizabeth is dying and receives Extreme Unction.

April 13   Good Friday, she is critical again.

April 14   Holy Saturday, sudden improvement.

May 13   Another serious attack; the sisters think she is dying.

May 24   Ascension. The Holy Trinity's presence felt in her soul, her "all-powerful Council."

May 25–June 2   Pentecost retreat.

July 8–9   After invoking Thérèse of Lisieux's help, Elizabeth can walk again.

Early August	*Heaven in Faith*, Elizabeth writes a ten-day retreat, as a souvenir for Guite.
August 16–31	*Last Retreat*, Elizabeth makes notes on her "novitiate for heaven."
August	*Greatness of Our Vocation*, a final letter to her friend, Françoise de Sourdon.
Oct./Nov.	*Let Yourself Be Loved*, a letter to Mother Germaine, found after Elizabeth's death.
Oct. 29	Last visit from her family.
Oct. 30	Elizabeth is confined to bed.
Oct. 31	She receives Extreme Unction for the second time.
Nov. 1	Feast of All Saints. Elizabeth receives Holy Communion for the last time.
Nov. 9	Elizabeth dies, after only five years in Carmel. Feast of the Lateran Basilica.
1931	
March 23/May	Cause of her beatification is introduced.
1961	
Oct. 25	Pope John XXIII gives papal approval for the cause to proceeed.
1984	
Feb. 17	Miracle attributed to the intercession of Sister Elizabeth is given papal approval. Father Jean Chanut, a Cistercian with tuberculosis, was completely healed after a novena of prayer to Sister Elizabeth of the Trinity offered by his own abbey of Citeaux and other Cistercian communities.
1984	
Nov. 25	Pope John Paul II beatifies Sister Elizabeth on the Solemnity of Christ the King.
2016	
March 3	Pope Francis approves the miracle needed for the canonization: the cure on April 2, 2002, of a Belgian woman, Marie-Paul Stevens, of Sjogren's disease, at the Carmel of Flavignerot, France.
Oct. 16	Pope Francis canonizes Elizabeth of the Trinity.

Bibliography

Primary Texts

Balthasar Hans Urs von. *Two Sisters in the Spirit; Thérèse of Lisieux and Elizabeth of the Trinity.* San Francisco: Ignatius Press, 1988.

Balthasar's book makes for prayerful reading, presenting a theological biography of these two holy Carmelites and the complementary nature of their spirituality. He focuses on Elizabeth's insights on the indwelling of God in the soul.

Bourges Carmel. *Les Mots d'Elizabeth de la Trinité Concordance.* Carmel Bourges & Carmel-EdiT, 2006.

A concordance of all Elizabeth's writings. Although in French, it still enables the reader to identify any quotation from Elizabeth. It opens with an excellent article by Conrad de Meester, "An Essay on Elizabeth the Writer."

De Meester, Conrad. *I Have Found God: Complete Works, Volume 1: General Introduction, Major Spiritual Writings.* Washington, DC: ICS Publications, 1984.

Conrad de Meester is the world authority on Elizabeth of the Trinity, responsible for the one-volume critical edition of her *Complete Works*, in French, which have been translated into English in 3 volumes. De Meester combines a panoramic knowledge of Elizabeth's context, life, and spirituality with a scholar's attention to detail.

———. *Elisabeth de la Trinité: Oeuvres Complètes.* Paris: Cerf, 2002.

———. *I Have Found God; Complete Works, Volume II: Letters from Carmel.* Washington, DC: 1995. *Third volume pending.*

Dijon Carmel. *The Praise of Glory: Reminiscences of Sr. Elizabeth of the Trinity.* Trans. Benedictine of Stanbrook. Cork: Mercier Press, 1913. This first biography, written by Mother Germaine of Jesus, Elizabeth's novice mistress and prioress, contains so many extracts from Elizabeth's *Diary* and *Letters* that it is virtually an autobiography. Although the style is somewhat sentimental and the events and writings are not chronological, obscuring Elizabeth's spiritual

163

development, it made Elizabeth known and loved and led to her cause being introduced in 1931.

Philipon M. M. *The Spiritual Doctrine of Sr. Elizabeth of the Trinity.* Cork: The Mercier Press, 1947.

Philipon describes his book as "a theologian's view of a soul and a doctrine." He gained unique insight into Elizabeth from his extensive conversations with both Mother Germaine and Marguerite, Elizabeth's younger sister. Like Mother Germaine, Philipon tends to overemphasize Elizabeth's spirituality at the expense of her humanity; however, his book provided the first doctrinal reflection on Elizabeth and renewed interest in her message.

Other Reading

Elizabeth of the Trinity and Columba Marmion. *Barb of Fire: Twenty Poems of Bl. Elizabeth of the Trinity with selected passages from Bl. Columba Marmion.* Trans. Alan Bancroft. Leominster: Gracewing, 2001.

A third of this book is devoted to a lively and illuminating introduction. Bancroft has sensitively translated Elizabeth's poems, cleverly capturing her rhyme and intent. His astute juxtaposition of passages from Marmion enhances the reader's appreciation of these two great contemplatives.

Borriello, Luigi. *Spiritual Doctrine of Blessed Elizabeth of the Trinity.* New York: Alba House, 1986.

This book traces the similarity between Elizabeth of the Trinity's doctrine and the teaching of Vatican Council II, especially in her emphasis on the universal call to holiness and prayer.

La France, Jean. *Elizabeth of the Trinity: The Charism of Her Prayer.* Darlington Carmel, 1983.

This beautiful book reflects on Elizabeth's understanding of her vocation as a "Praise of Glory," elaborating on her description from *Heaven in Faith* given in this anthology.

Moorcroft, Jennifer. *He is My Heaven: The Life of Elizabeth of the Trinity.* Washington, DC: ICS, 2001.

Moorcroft's very readable biography provides an insight into late nineteenth-century France, the context in which Elizabeth, a musically gifted and humanly attractive young woman, developed such a profound spirituality.

Mosley, Joanne. *Elizabeth of the Trinity: The Unfolding of Her Message.* Vol. 1: *In the World and In Community.* Oxford: Teresian Press, 2012.

———. *Elizabeth of the Trinity: The Unfolding of Her Message.* Vol. 2: *In the Infirmary and After Her Death.* Oxford: Teresian Press, 2012.

In this comprehensive new biography, Joanne Mosley offers a fact-filled, engaging, and inspiring account of Elizabeth's life spanning the years before her entrance to Carmel through her death and beyond. This new two-volume set may easily become the definitive non-translated biography published in English.

Murphy, M. T. *The Vast Triangled Heart: The Life and Spirituality of Elizabeth of the Trinity.* Leominster, England: Gracewing, 2011.

CDs

Two sets of compact discs of talks on Elizabeth of the Trinity, given by the author and recorded live at the Carmel of Liverpool, England. May be ordered from the Carmelite Book Service, Oxford, England: *http://www.carmelite.org.uk/acatalog/Online Catalogue BL ELIZABETH OF THE TRINITY 101.html.*

Set I

Talk 1 Elizabeth of the Trinity. Life Before Carmel, 1880–1901. (Ref. 9782) $7.20

Talk 2 Elizabeth of the Trinity: Life in Carmel, 1901–1906. (Ref. 9783) $7.20

Talk 3 Elizabeth of the Trinity: Elizabeth's Spirituality, especially "Let Yourself Be Loved." (Ref 9784) $7.20

Set II (2008)

Talk 1 Elizabeth of the Trinity: Baptism and the Trinity. (Ref. 9778) $7.20

Talk 2 Elizabeth of the Trinity: Eucharist. (Ref 9779) $7.20

Talk 3 Elizabeth of the Trinity: Teaching on Prayer. (Ref 9780). $7.20

Talk 4: Elizabeth of the Trinity and St. Paul. (Ref. 9781) $7.20

Acknowledgments

I wish to express my sincere gratitude to Alan Bancroft. He has been unstinting in his encouragement, practical help, and poems. His gift of an early edition of *Souvenirs* (Carmel de Dijon, 1913) furnished the material from which I translated this selection. I sought to produce a new translation, but drew widely on the classic translation of the Stanbrook community, whose kindness I wish to acknowledge.

Poems of Elizabeth of the Trinity, translation copyright Alan Bancroft, are taken from *Barb of Fire* (Gracewing, Leominster, 2001) and are used with permission of the publisher.

Warm thanks to Sister Marie-Michelle de la Croix, O.C.D., of Dijon Carmel at Flavignerot for her help and prayer, and to the community for permission to use photos of Elizabeth and brief extracts from her death circular.

Thanks to Tom Masters and Gary Brandl, editor and publisher respectively at New City Press, whose skills and suggestions were invaluable in arranging for the publication of the New City Press Edition in 2009.

And thanks to ICS Publications, the Discalced Carmelite publishing ministry in the United States, and to Patricia Lynn Morrison, ICS editorial director. Their enthusiasm and support has given this book new life as one of their titles, helping to promote awareness of the spirituality of the newly canonized Elizabeth.

From the outset, the prioress and community at Liverpool Carmel were greatly supportive of this work, and to them I express my deep gratitude.

About Us

ICS Publications, based in Washington, D.C., is the publishing house of the Institute of Carmelite Studies (ICS) and a ministry of the Discalced Carmelite Friars of the Washington Province (U.S.A.). The Institute of Carmelite Studies promotes research and publication in the field of Carmelite spirituality, especially about Carmelite saints and related topics. Its members are friars of the Washington Province.

The Discalced Carmelites are a worldwide Roman Catholic religious order comprised of friars, nuns, and laity—men and women who are heirs to the teaching and way of life of Teresa of Avila and John of the Cross, dedicated to contemplation and to ministry in the church and the world.

Information about their way of life is available through local diocesan vocation offices, or from the Discalced Carmelite Friars vocation directors at the following addresses:

Washington Province:
1525 Carmel Road, Hubertus, WI 53033

California-Arizona Province:
P.O. Box 3420, San Jose, CA 95156

Oklahoma Province:
5151 Marylake Drive, Little Rock, AR 72206

Visit our websites at:
www.icspublications.org and *http://ocdfriarsvocation.org*